The Requirements of Writing

The Requirements of Writing

Robert Rennie LLB, PhD
Professor of Conveyancing, University of Glasgow, Solicitor

D J Cusine LLB, NP
Professor of Conveyancing and
Professional Practice of Law, University of Aberdeen

Butterworths
Law Society of Scotland

Edinburgh   1995

95- 133551 (2)

United Kingdom	Butterworths a division of Reed Elsevier (UK) Ltd, 4 Hill Street, EDINBURGH EH2 3JZ and Halsbury House, 35 Chancery Lane, LONDON WC2A 1EL
Australia	Butterworths, SYDNEY, MELBOURNE, BRISBANE, ADELAIDE, PERTH, CANBERRA and HOBART
Canada	Butterworths Canada Ltd, TORONTO and VANCOUVER
Ireland	Butterworth (Ireland) Ltd, DUBLIN
Malaysia	Malayan Law Journal Sdn Bhd, KUALA LUMPUR
New Zealand	Butterworths of New Zealand Ltd, WELLINGTON and AUCKLAND
Puerto Rico	Butterworths of Puerto Rico Inc, SAN JUAN
Singapore	Butterworths Asia, SINGAPORE
South Africa	Butterworth Publishers (Pty) Ltd, DURBAN
USA	Butterworth Legal Publishers, CARLSBAD, California, and SALEM, New Hampshire

Law Society of Scotland
26 Drumsheugh Gardens, EDINBURGH EH3 7YR

A CIP Catalogue record for this book is available from the British Library.

ISBN 0 406 06331 1

Typeset by Phoenix Photosetting, Chatham, Kent
Printed and bound in Great Britain by Mackays of Chatham PLC, Kent

Preface

The Requirements of Writing (Scotland) Act 1995 has been a long time in the gestation. It emanates from a Scottish Law Commission Report which was published in 1988. Although a Bill was introduced in 1989 it fell for procedural reasons, but a similar, although not identical, Bill is now the Act. The Act came about because of a feeling that some of the law on the execution and proof of obligations was out-of-date or unclear and, in some cases, could work unjustly, for example in relation to notarial executions.

While what follows could not be described as a bumper book of fun, we have tried to explain the Act and, wherever possible, indicate its practical effects. However as the law prior to the Act will still be relevant for years, if not centuries, to come, there is a chapter on it also and we hope that the inclusion of both will provide a minor *vade mecum* to the law.

The 1995 Act is included as an appendix, as are the relevant sections of the 1874 Act and 1970 Act and the older Scots Acts which have stood us in good stead, in some cases for over 300 years, and in others for over 400.

In producing this account of the law we have benefited from lectures given by D J McNeil (the other 'D J') and from discussions with *inter alios* David Bennett and Ian Jamieson. The manuscript was typed by Maureen Mercer and Amanda Walton in Aberdeen and by Gillian Guthrie, Mary Love and Jean Steele in Glasgow and Motherwell, for whose assistance we are most grateful.

The law is stated as at 1 May 1995 and we have made absolutely no attempt to take account of subsequent developments.

Adopted as holograph   Adopted as holograph

Contents

Preface   *v*
Table of statutes   *ix*
Table of cases   *xiii*
Abbreviations   *xvii*

CHAPTER 1
Historical background   1

CHAPTER 2
The law prior to 1995   15

CHAPTER 3
The law after 1995 – execution by individuals   43

CHAPTER 4
The law after 1995 – execution of deeds by persons other
than natural persons   71

CHAPTER 5
Repeals and amendments   79

Appendices   83

Index   139

Table of statutes

PARA

Age of Legal Capacity (Scotland) Act 1991 (c 50) 2.12

Blank Bonds and Trusts Act
  1696 (c 25) 2.23, 5.02
Building Societies Act 1986
  (c 53) 2.09

Church of Scotland (Property
  and Endowments) Amend-
  ment Act 1933 (c 44)
  s 13 .... 2.31, 5.02
Companies Act 1908 (c 69) ... 1.07
Companies Act 1948 (c 38) ... 2.10
Companies Act 1985 (c 6) .. 4.04, 5.06
  s 26 .... 2.11
    27 .... 2.11
    36(3) 2.10
    36B 2.10, 4.04
    39(3) 5.06
    40(2) 5.06
    186(2) 5.06
    188(2) 5.06
    283(3) 4.03
    654 .... 2.11
Companies Act 1989 (c 40)
  s 130 .... 2.10
Conveyancing and Feudal
  Reform (Scotland) Act
  1970 (c 35) 1.12, 2.03, 5.03
  s 44 .... 1.07, 1.11, 2.03, 5.02
Conveyancing (Scotland) Act
  1874 (c 94) 1.11, 2.02,
          2.28, 2.29, 2.31, 5.03
  ss 38–41 .... 5.02
    38 .... 1.07, 1.11, 2.12,
           2.16, 2.24
    39 .... 1.07, 1.13, 2.27,
           2.28, 2.30, 2.33
    40 .... 2.35
  Schs 2.31
Conveyancing (Scotland) Act
  1924 (c 27) 2.29, 5.03
  s 18 .... 2.31, 3.32, 3.34, 5.02
    (1) 2.31

PARA

Conveyancing (Scotland) Act
  1924—contd
  Schs 2.31
  Sch 1 .... 2.32, 5.02

Deeds Act 1696 (c 15) 1.09, 1.10,
        1.16, 2.02, 2.29, 5.02

Execution of Deeds Act 1593
  (c 179) 1.08, 1.09, 2.02

Form of Deeds Act 1856 (c 89): 1.11

Housing (Scotland) Act 1987
  (c 26)
  s 53(1) 5.03
    54(6) 5.03

Insolvency Act 1986 (c 45)
  s 53 .... 5.06
  Sch 1,
    para 9 .... 4.03, 4.04
  Sch 2,
    para 9 .... 4.03, 4.04
  Sch 4, ... 4.04
    para 7 .... 4.03

Land Registration (Scotland)
  Act 1979 (c 33)
  s 4(1) 1.14, 3.30
Lands Clauses Consolidation
  (Scotland) Act 1845 (c 19): 5.03
Law Reform (Miscellaneous
  Provisions) (Scotland) Act
  1985 (c 73)
  s 8 .... 1.02
Law Reform (Miscellaneous
  Provisions) (Scotland) Act
  1990 (c 40)
  s 72 .... 2.10
Local Government (Scotland)
  Act 1947 (c 43) 2.08
  s 194 .... 2.08
Local Government (Scotland)
  Act 1973 (c 65)
  s 235(1) 4.06

	PARA
Local Government etc (Scotland) Act 1994 (c 39)	
s 2	4.06
Lord Lyon King of Arms Act 1672 (c 47)	2.06
Mercantile Law Amendment Act (Scotland) 1856 (c 60)	
s 6	5.02
Partnership Act 1890 (c 39)	
s 2	4.02
5	2.07, 4.02
6	4.02
Patents Act 1977 (c 37)	
s 31(6)	5.03
Prescription and Limitation (Scotland) Act 1973 (c 52)	
s 5	5.02
Sch 1,	
para 2	5.02
(e)	5.02
para 3	5.02
para 4(b)	5.02
Registration of Leases (Scotland) Act 1857 (c 26)	5.03
Requirements of Writing (Scotland) Act 1995 (c 7):	1.01, 1.04, 1.06, 1.08, 1.14, 1.16, 2.01, 2.03, 2.32, 2.34, 2.39, 2.40, 4.01, 4.02
s 1	3.01, 3.02
(2)	3.02
(a)(i)–(iii)	3.02
(b), (c)	3.02
(3)	3.03
(4)	3.03, 3.07
(5)	3.03, 3.08, 3.09
(6)	3.03, 3.04
(7)	3.10
(a)–(c)	3.10
(8)(a), (b)	3.10
2(1)	1.06, 3.02, 3.11
(2)	3.02
3	3.28, 3.29, 3.30, 5.05
(1)	3.18, 3.24, 3.35, 4.03
(b)	3.35, 4.06
(c)	4.06
(1A)	4.06
(1B)	4.07
(2)	3.11, 3.12, 3.18
(3)	3.19, 3.25, 3.37

	PARA
Requirements of Writing (Scotland) Act 1995—*contd*	
s 3(4)(a)	3.20, 3.25
(b)	3.21
(c)(i)–(iii)	3.21
(d)	3.21, 3.22, 3.25
(e)	3.23, 3.25
(f)	3.25
(g)	3.25, 4.06
(h)	4.04
(5)	3.21
(6)	3.23
(7)	3.22
(8)	3.24
(10)	3.24
4	3.28, 3.29, 3.30, 5.05
(1)	3.32
(a), (b)	3.28
(2)(a), (b)	3.28
(3), (4)	3.28
(5)	3.28, 3.29
(a)	3.28
(6)(b)	3.28
5(1)(a), (b)	3.39
(2)(a), (b)	3.41
(3)	3.39
(5)	3.39, 3.42
(6), (7)	3.39
6	1.06, 3.29, 3.32
(1)	3.29
(2)	3.29, 5.03
(3)	3.29
(a), (b)	3.29
(c)(i)–(iv)	3.29
(d)	3.29
(4)	3.29
7(1)	3.11
(2)(a)–(c)	3.12
(3), (4)	3.13
(5)	3.21, 3.26
(6)	3.15
8(1)–(6)	3.27
9	3.32
(1)	3.34
(b)	3.32
(2)	3.32, 3.35
(4)	3.36
(5)	3.35
(6)	3.33
(7)	3.32
10(1), (2)	3.37
11	3.04
(1), (2)	3.38
(3)(a)	3.38

PARA

Requirements of Writing (Scotland) Act 1995—*contd*
s 12 .... 4.04
    (1) 4.04
    (2) 3.17
13 .... 3.15
Sch 1,
  para 1(1) 4.04
      (a), (b) 4.04, 4.06
      (c) 4.06
    (2) 3.40
    (4)(h) 4.06
    (1A), (1C) 4.04
  para 2 .... 3.40
Sch 2,
  para 2(1) 4.01, 4.02
    (2) 4.01
    (3) 4.02
  3 .... 4.02, 4.03
    (1) 4.01, 4.03, 4.04
    (2) 4.04
    (3) 4.03
    (5) 4.04
     (a) 4.03
    (6) 4.03, 4.04
  4(1) 4.01, 4.06
    (2), (3) 4.06
    (5)–(8) 4.06
  5 .... 4.04
    (2) 4.01, 4.07
    (a)–(c) 4.07
    (3)–(8) 4.07
  6 .... 4.08
    (1) 4.01
    (a)–(d) 4.08
    (2) 4.08
    (4) 4.08
    (6), (7) 4.08
Sch 3 .... 3.32
  para 2 .... 3.35
  para 4(dd) 3.32
Sch 4 .... 5.06
  paras 38–40 .... 5.05

PARA

Requirements of Writing (Scotland) Act 1995—*contd*
Sch 4—*contd*
  paras 53–55 .... 5.06
  para 58 .... 5.06
Sch 5 .... 1.16, 5.06
Reversion Act 1555 (c 29) .. 1.08, 1.09

Subscription of Deeds Act
  1540 (c 117) 1.08, 1.16,
            2.01, 2.02, 2.29,
            2.31, 5.02
Subscription of Deeds Act
  1579 (c 80) 1.08, 1.09,
            1.16, 2.01, 2.02,
            2.31, 5.02
Subscription of Deeds Act
  1584 (c 4) 1.08, 2.02
Subscription of Deeds Act
  1681 (c 5) 1.09, 1.16,
            2.01, 2.02, 2.29,
            2.31, 5.02
Succession (Scotland) Act 1964
  (c 41) 5.03
s 21 .... 2.35, 5.05
  21A 5.05
  24 .... 3.28
  32 .... 5.05

Titles to Land Consolidation
  (Scotland) Act 1868 (c 101): 2.24,
            5.03
  s 149 .... 5.02
Transmission of Moveable
  Property (Scotland) Act
  1862 (c 85) 5.03
Trusts (Scotland) Act 1921
  (c 58) 5.03

Wills Act 1963 (c 44) 2.44
  s 1 .... 2.44
  2(1)(a), (c) 2.44
  6(1) 2.44

Table of cases

Abernethy v Forbes (1835) 13 S 263 .... 2.22
Aitken 1965 SLT (Sh Ct) 15 .... 2.31
Allan and Crichton, Petitioners 1933 SLT (Sh Ct) 2 .... 2.06
American Express v Royal Bank 1989 SLT 650 .... 2.06
Anderson v Gill (1858) 20 D 1326 .... 1.03
Ayrshire Hospice, Petitioners 1993 SLT (Sh Ct) 75 .... 2.05

Baird's Trustees v Baird 1955 SC 286 .... 2.05, 2.15, 2.29
Bisset, Petitioner 1961 SLT (Sh Ct) 19 .... 2.27, 2.30
Blair v Assets Company (1896) 25 R (HL) 36 .... 2.15
Bogie's Executors v Bogie 1953 SLT (Sh Ct) 32 .... 2.05, 2.30
Boswell v Boswell (1852) 14 D 378 .... 2.18
Boyd v Shaw 1927 SC 414 .... 2.14
Bridgeford's Executor v Bridgeford 1948 SC 416 .... 2.37
Brock v Brock 1908 SC 964 .... 2.12, 3.21
Brown (1883) 11 R 400 .... 2.30
Brown v Duncan (1888) 15 R 511 .... 2.06, 2.28
Buchan (Earl of) v Scottish Widows Fund Society (1857) 19 D 551 .... 2.22

Chisholm v Chisholm 1949 SC 434 .... 2.38
Clydesdale Bank (Moore Place) Nominees Ltd v Snodgrass 1939 SC 805 .. 2.10
Craig v Richardson (1610) Mor 16829 .... 3.36
Crawford's Trustees v Glasgow Royal Infirmary 1955 SC 367 .... 2.31, 3.36
Crosbie v Picken (1749) Mor 16814 .... 2.06

Danish Dairy Co v Gillespie 1922 SC 656 .... 3.05, 3.06
Dickson's Trustees v Goodall (1820) Hume 924 .... 2.26
Donaldson v Donaldson (1749) Mor 9080 .... 2.23
Draper v Thomason 1954 SC 136 .... 2.06
Duff v Earl of Fife (1823) 1 Sh App 498 .... 2.31, 3.32
Dunlop v Greenlees' Trustees (1863) 2 M 1 .... 2.06

East Kilbride Development Corporation v Pollok 1953 SC 370 .... 3.04
Elliot's Executors 1939 SLT 69 .... 2.30
Errol v Walker 1966 SC 93 .... 3.09
Ewen v Ewen's Trustees (1830) 4 W & S 346, HL 2.22

Ferguson, Petitioner 1959 SC 56 .... 2.05, 2.06, 2.30
Ferrie v Ferrie's Trustees (1863) 1 M 291 .... 2.31, 3.36
Finlay v Finlay's Trustees 1948 SC 16 .... 2.31, 3.36
Forrest v Low's Trustees 1907 SC 1240 .... 2.14, 3.25

Gardner v Lucas (1877) 5 R 638 .... 3.06
Gardner v Lucas (1878) 5 R (HL) 105 .... 2.06
Gatty v Maclaine 1921 SC (HL) 1 .... 3.08
Gibson's Trustees v Lamb 1931 SLT 22 .... 2.15

Gillies v Glasgow Royal Infirmary 1960 SC 438 .... 2.37
Gorrie's Trustees v Stiven's Executrix 1952 SC 1 .... 2.31, 3.36
Graeme v Graeme's Trustees (1869) 7 M 1062 .... 3.36
Gray v Earl of Selkirk (1709) Robert 1 .... 2.35
Grieve's Trustees v Japp's Trustees 1917 1 SLT 70 .... 2.06, 2.28

Harvey v Smith (1904) 6 F 511 .... 2.38
Heiton v Waverley Hydropathic Co (1877) 4 R 830 .... 3.06
Hynd's Trustee v Hynd's Trustees 1955 SC (HL) 1 .... 2.13, 2.31, 2.32, 3.23

Inglis v Buttery & Co (1877) 5 R 58, affd (1878) 5 R (HL) 87 .... 1.02
Irvine v McHardy (1892) 19 R 458 .... 2.29

Keanie v Keanie 1940 SC 549 .... 3.07

Lang v Lang's Trustees (1889) 16 R 590 .... 2.31, 3.36
Lindsay v Milne 1995 SLT 487 .... 2.13
Littlejohn v MacKay 1974 SLT (Sh Ct) 82 .... 2.07, 4.02
Lorimer's Executors v Hird 1959 SLT (Notes) 8 .... 2.35
Lowrie's Judicial Factor v McMillan 1972 SC 105 .... 2.35

McArthur v McArthur's Executors 1931 SLT 463 .... 2.14
M'Beath's Trustees v M'Beath 1935 SC 471 .... 2.38
M'Dougall v M'Dougall (1875) 2 R 814 .... 2.17, 2.19
MacDougall v MacDougall's Executors 1994 SLT 1178 .... 2.13
McGinn v Shearer 1947 SC 334 .... 1.13, 2.39
McGuiness v Black (No 2) 1990 SLT 461, OH 4.05
McIldowie v Muller 1979 SC 271 .... 2.31
Maclaine v Murphy 1958 SLT (Sh Ct) 49 .... 2.38
McLaren v Menzies (1876) 3 R 1151 .... 2.30
M'Lay v Farrell 1950 SC 149 .... 2.05
McNeill v McNeill 1973 SLT (Sh Ct) 16 .... 2.30
Macrorie's Executors v McLaren 1982 SLT 295, OH 2.39
Manson v Edinburgh Royal Institution 1948 SLT 196 .... 2.35
Millar v Farquharson (1835) 13 S 838 .... 2.35
Milne's Executor v Waugh 1913 SC 203 .... 2.36
Mitchell v Miller (1742) Mor 16900 .... 2.12
Mitchell v Stornoway Trustees 1936 SC (HL) 56 .... 3.04
Moncrieff v Lawrie (1896) 23 R 577 .... 2.29
Moncrieff v Monypenny (1710) Mor 15936 .... 2.06
Mowat v Caledonian Banking Co (1895) 23 R 270 .... 3.05
Munro v Butler Johnstone (1868) 7 M 250 .... 2.20

Newstead v Dansken 1918 1 SLT 136, OH 2.31, 3.36
Noble v Noble (1875) 3 R 74 .... 2.06
Norval v Abbey 1939 SC 724 .... 1.02

Ormistoun v Hamilton (1708) Mor 16890 .... 2.12

Paterson v Paterson (1897) 25 R 144 .... 1.04
Pattison's Trustees v the University of Edinburgh (1886) 16 R 73, OH .. 2.25, 3.41
Perkikou v Pattison 1958 SLT 153 .... 1.02
Pollock v Whiteford 1936 SC 402 .... 3.05
Purvis's Trustees v Purvis's Executors (1861) 23 D 812 .... 2.43

Table of cases

Reid v Kedder (1840) 1 Robin 183, HL 2.18, 2.20
Rhodes v Peterson 1972 SLT 198 .... 2.06
Richardson's Trustees (1891) 18 R 1131 .... 2.30
Robertson v Ogilvie's Trustees (1844) 7 D 236 .... 2.36
Rutterford Ltd v Allied Breweries 1990 SLT 249 .... 3.07

Scottish Provident Institution v Cohen (1886) 16 R 112 .... 2.42
Secretary of State for Scotland v Ravenstone Securities Ltd 1976 SC 171 .. 3.05
Shiell 1936 SLT 317 .... 2.30
Sibbald v Sibbald (1776) Mor 16906 .... 3.25
Simson v Simson (1883) 10 R 1247 .... 2.12
Smith v Bank of Scotland (1824) 2 Sh App 265, HL 3.25
Smith v Chambers' Trustees (1878) 5 R (HL) 151 .... 2.15
Smyth v Smyth (1876) 3 R 573 .... 2.29
Stephen v Scott 1927 SC 85 .... 2.31
Stirling Stuart v Stirling Crawfurd's Trustees (1885) 12 R 610 .... 2.06
Stobo Ltd v Morrisons (Gowns) Ltd 1949 SC 184 .... 3.04
Syme's Executors v Cherrie 1986 SLT 161, OH 2.25

Tait's Trustees v Chiene 1911 SC 743 .... 2.35
Taylor's Executrices v Thom 1914 SC 79 .... 2.05, 2.35
Temperance Permanent Building Society v Kominek 1951 SLT (Sh Ct) 58 . 3.04
Thomson's Trustees v Bowhill Baptist Church 1956 SC 217 .... 2.25
Thomson's Trustees v Easson (1878) 6 R 141 .... 2.30
Tucker v Canch's Trustee 1953 SC 270 .... 2.37

Veasey v Malcolm's Trustees (1875) 2 R 748 .... 2.28
Veitch v Horsburgh (1637) M 16834 .... 2.31

Walker v Whitwell 1916 SC (HL) 75 .... 2.13, 2.29, 3.23
Waterson's Trustees v St Giles Boys' Club 1943 SC 369 .... 2.39

Abbreviations

Cases

D	Dunlop's Session Cases
F	Fraser's Session Cases
Hume	Hume's Decisions (Court of Session)
M	Macpherson's Session Cases
Mor	Morison's Dictionary of Decisions (Court of Session)
R	Rettie's Session Cases
R (HL)	House of Lords cases in Rettie's Session Cases
Robert	Robertson's Scotch Appeals (House of Lords)
Robin	Robinson's Scotch Appeals (House of Lords)
S	P Shaw's Session Cases
SC	Session Cases
SC (HL)	House of Lords cases in Session Cases
SLT	Scots Law Times
SLT (Sh Ct)	Sheriff Court Reports in Scots Law Times
Sh App	P Shaw's Scotch Appeals (House of Lords)
W & S	Wilson and Shaw's House of Lords Cases

Textbooks

Cusine and Rennie	*Missives* (1993, Butterworths Law Society of Scotland)
Erskine	*Institute of the Law of Scotland* (2 vols, 1773)
Gloag	*The Law of Contract* (2nd edn, 1929)
Halliday	*Conveyancing Law and Practice in Scotland* (1985, W Green)
McBryde	*The Law of Contract in Scotland* (1987, W Green)
Walker and Walker	*The Law of Evidence in Scotland* (1964, T & T Clark)

CHAPTER 1

Historical background

The need for a system

1.01 Fundamental to any system of conveyancing is the need for a coherent set of principles regulating the execution of deeds. Conveyancing as a subject is very often described as that body of law which deals with the creation, transfer, variation and extinction of rights and obligations by formal deed. In his introductory lecture delivered in 1856 Alexander Montgomery Bell, Professor of Conveyancing in the University of Edinburgh described his task in the following terms:

'The province of the Chair of Conveyancing is to impart a scientific and practical acquaintance with the Scottish system of deeds, – that is, of the writings by which in this country obligations and rights are constituted and perfected, – to explain their origin in history, their styles or forms, their peculiarities of adaptation to particular circumstances, the solemnities of their execution, and the requisites to their efficacy after being completed in point of form.'

Professor Halliday in his more recent treatise[1] described conveyancing as:

'That branch of law which deals with the preparation of deeds. It is the body of law and procedure which relates to the constitution, transfer and discharge by written documents of rights and obligations in connection with property of all kinds.'

If, therefore, private law is the substance or 'what' of the law and jurisprudence and allied philosophical subjects the 'why' of the law, conveyancing is the 'how' of the law. One might say that conveyancing is carried out in the engine room of the law. The manner in which writings are executed and whether or not that execution is sufficient to endow them with the

1

status of a probative writ is an important branch of conveyancing. With the passing of the Requirements of Writing (Scotland) Act 1995 our system of execution of deeds has undergone a radical transformation.

1 Halliday *Conveyancing Law and Practice in Scotland* (1985) vol I, para 1–01.

Formal validity and essential validity

1.02 Any discussion of the concept of probativity and the solemnities laid down by law in relation to the execution of deeds must begin with an understanding of the difference between essential validity and formal validity. As a formal matter a written document may be perfectly valid in accordance with the law but still require to be spoken to as a matter of evidence or proof. A probative writing on the other hand is a document which *in addition* to being validly executed proves itself and its contents without any need for further evidence. Indeed as the law stands at the moment there is a general rule to the effect that extrinsic evidence to contradict or vary the contents of a probative deed is inadmissible unless there is some patent ambiguity. Lord Gifford stated in the leading case of *Inglis v Buttery*[1] 'where parties agreed to embody and do actually embody their contract in a formal written deed, then in determining what the contract really was . . . a court must look to the formal deed and to that deed alone.'

Any person who seeks to challenge or disprove the provisions of a probative deed can, subject to the power of the court to rectify a defectively expressed document in terms of the Law Reform (Miscellaneous Provisions) (Scotland) Act 1985, s 8, do so only by a formal action of reduction in which the onus of proof rests firmly on the person seeking the reduction[2]. In practice lawyers use the term probative in two distinct senses: one relates to the formal constitution of the deed where that deed must be probative to be validly constituted and the other relates purely to evidential quality of the deed as it stands.

1 *Inglis v Buttery & Co* (1877) 5 R 58 at 69; affd (1877) 5 R (HL) 87; see also *Norval v Abbey* 1939 SC 724; *Perkikou v Pattison* 1958 SLT 153.
2 See Walker and Walker *The Law of Evidence in Scotland* (1964) p 181.

Privileged writings

1.03 Certain writings were accorded the status of probative writings even though they did not comply with the authentication statutes in that they were not witnessed. It is perhaps incorrect to treat holograph writings and writings adopted as holograph in the same category as writing *in re mercatoria*. Nevertheless, these types of writings are all generally regarded as privileged. Holograph writings were not in themselves probative because it was still required to be proved that the document was in the handwriting of the grantor and subscribed by him or her[1]. Nevertheless, they were generally treated as probative for the purposes of satisfying the constitutive requirements of the *obligationes literis*[2]. It is not necessary to discuss documents *in re mercatoria* in any great detail. Suffice it to say that any contract or deed relative to heritable property was not a document *in re mercatoria*.

1 *Anderson v Gill* (1858) 20 D 1326.
2 For a general discussion of the requirements of holograph writing see *Halliday* vol I, paras 3–52 ff; Cusine and Rennie *Missives* (1993) paras 2.01 to 2.05.

Obligationes literis

1.04 Prior to the passing of the Requirements of Writing (Scotland) Act 1995, obligations tended to fall into one of three different categories. The categories derived from the decision in *Paterson v Paterson*[1]. These categories were:
(1) *Obligationes literis*, where the contract or obligation had to be constituted in probative writing or, as an alternative, in holograph writing for its essential validity.
(2) Obligations or contracts which as a matter of proof required writing or the oath of the party seeking to challenge the same but which could be constituted in any way.
(3) Obligations or contracts which could be constituted orally and also proved *prout de jure*[2].

1 (1897) 25 R 144.
2 For a general discussion of these categories and in particular the category of *obligationes literis* see Gloag *The Law of Contract* (2nd edn, 1929) Ch X; McBryde *The Law of Contract in Scotland* (1987) paras 27–05 ff.

1.05 Contracts or deeds which fell into the category of *obligationes literis* required probative or privileged writing to be validly constituted, or alternatively an informal agreement or oral agreement followed by homologation or *rei interventus*[1]. The question of which contracts were included in the category of *obligationes literis* is a matter of some doubt, at least as regards the peripheral contracts. Gloag listed contracts relating to heritage; contracts of service for more than a year; contracts for the transfer of incorporeals; contracts of insurance; cautionary obligations; contracts of mandate; contracts for the sale or mortgage of a ship[2]. Of these seven categories cautionary obligations, contracts of insurance and transfers of incorporeals are stated to be doubtful inclusions in the category by the authors of a leading work on evidence[3]. There is no doubt that the principal contracts included in the category were contracts relating to heritage including securities, but excepting leases for not more than a year, and contracts of service for more than a year[4].

1 For a general discussion of *rei interventus* and homologation see *Cusine and Rennie* paras 2.06 ff.
2 *Contract* p 162.
3 *Walker and Walker* p 85.
4 *Halliday* vol I, para 3–02 and *McBryde* para 27–08.

The authentication statutes

1.06 Prior to the passing of the 1995 Act, for a deed to be probative it had to comply with a series of statutes known as the authentication statutes. Although the 1995 Act has abolished or modified many of the existing formalities it has retained the concept of probativity in the sense that a document is self-proving. While s 2(1) of the Act makes it clear that subscription alone is required for a deed to be valid, s 6 looks back to the concept of an *obligatio literis* by retaining the requirement that certain deeds and documents must be probative if they are to enter the Register of Sasines or the Books of Council and Session or sheriff court books. In a sense the historical tradition of the authentication statutes, whereby a deed was probative if the subscription was attested by witnessing, has been maintained, although all the old authentication statutes have been repealed.

1.07 It cannot be denied that the 1995 Act has a certain inner consistency comparable with the very oldest of the statutes. In one sense it can be argued that the new provisions for execution of deeds by limited companies which allow probativity to be achieved by a single witness to a single signature are more akin to the original authentication statutes than all the statutory provisions for company execution from at least the Companies Act 1908 onwards. The original authentication statutes were enacted in the sixteenth and seventeenth centuries. Up to the passing of the 1995 Act, these Acts remained in force subject to various amendments in later nineteenth and twentieth century legislation[1]. The rationale behind the requirement of authentication is and always has been commercial. Scots law has long recognised the importance of certainty in relation to deeds and other written documents and from early days statutes have laid down provisions in relation to the attestation of witnessing of the execution of a deed. Because a witness signs a deed, the signature of the granter is stated to be attested. Stair justified the statutory solemnities as allowing parties 'to enjoy their rights not only in safety and security, but in confidence and quietness of mind, that they may clearly know what is their right, and may securely enjoy the same'[2].

1 Conveyancing (Scotland) Act 1874, ss 38, 39; Conveyancing and Feudal Reform (Scotland) Act 1970, s 44.
2 *Institutions*, I, 1, 15.

1.08 The earliest form of execution in Scotland appears to have been by cross or mark. In the earliest times there is evidence of the execution of charters by King Duncan II by making a cross with other crosses made by his brother and witnesses. Soon thereafter the practice of the adhibition of the granter's seal came into being both in relation to Crown charters and private documents. Sealing carried with it the risk of fraud and the practice does not appear to have been controlled in any particular way, with parties using seals lent by others in certain cases. The writs or deeds themselves were generally written out by a churchman or, in the words of Professor Montgomery Bell, 'churchmen-notaries'[1]. It appears to be the case that such men were not wholly to be trusted and in

1540, during the last years of the reign of James V, the Scottish Parliament passed what is now known as the Subscription of Deeds Act 1540[2].

'That therefor na faith be gevin in toime cuing to ony obligatioun band or uther writting under ane seale without the subscription of him that awe the salmin, and witnesse: or else gif the party cannot write with the subscription of ane Notar thereto.'

The Subscription of Deeds Act 1540 is remarkably short, but, like many of the old Scottish Acts, it achieved a great deal with few words. In effect it laid down three principal rules in relation to execution of deeds:
(1) the deed must be subscribed by the granter;
(2) witnesses are required; and
(3) if the granter cannot write a notary can sign for that party.
The difficulty with the Act was that it did not specify in any great detail what the witnesses were actually to do, and it did not say in so many words that the witnesses required to sign the deed as well as actually witness the subscription of the granter. The general practice appears to have been that the witnesses were specified in the deed but did not necessarily sign[3]. Matters were again addressed by the Scottish Parliament in 1555[4] in an Act 'against the sealing and subscription of reversions and writs belangand thereto' which prescribed sealing and subscription by the granter with those unable to write being able to have their hand led at the pen by a notary. This Act which was passed during the reign of Mary Queen of Scots and the regency of Mary of Guise did nothing to clarify the position of the witnesses, although it did clarify what was required of the notary where a party could not write. The fact that it did not mention witnesses at all supports the view that the witnesses were not intended to subscribe under the Act of 1540[5]. In 1579, during the reign of James VI, the Subscription of Deeds Act was passed to clarify matters. This Act applied to heritable property and deeds of great importance and was designed in the main to prevent improper conduct on the part of notaries.

'That all contractes, obligationes, reversiones, assignationes, and discharges of reversiones or eikes thereto, and generally all writs importing heritabil title or utheris bands and obligationes of great importance, to be maid in all time comming, sal be subscrived

and seilled be the principal parties, gif they can subscrive, uther-
wise be twa famous notars befoir four famous witnesses, denomi-
tnat by their special dwellingplace or sum other evident tokens,
that the witnesses be non knawen, being present at that time,
otherwise the saides writs to mak na faith.'

The Act of 1584[6] dispensed with sealing where the writ was
registered for preservation in the court books, as that was
regarded as a greater solemnity than sealing. After 1584 the
practice of sealing gradually ceased in the case of all solemnly
executed deeds, whether registered or not. The Act of 1593[7]
added the requirement for the insertion of the name and designation of the writer of the deed at the end, before the insertion of
the witnesses. The Act of 1593 re-emphasised the main function
of the law of authentication in relation to probative deeds,
namely, to make forgery more difficult. The Act states:

'Falsettes increasis daily within this realm; and specially, be the
writing of the bodies of the contractes, chartouris, obligationes,
reversiones, assignationes, and all utheris, writtes and eviden-
tes, be the hand-writtes of sick persons as are not knawen.'

Like previous Acts before it, the Act of 1593 provides a
sanction for non-compliance with its requirement, which is that
the writ in question shall 'mak na faith'. The notion of a writ
'making faith' is, of course, at the very heart of the notion of probativity. A probative writ was and, even after the passing of the
1995 Act, is a writ which makes faith and proves itself.

1 *Lectures on Conveyancing* (1882) vol 1, p 28.
2 Act of 1540, c 117 (Subscription of Deeds).
3 Erskine *An Institute of the Law of Scotland* (8th edn, 1871) III, 2, 7.
4 Act of 1555, c 29 (Reversions).
5 *Montgomery Bell* vol I, p 29.
6 c 4 (Subscription of Deeds).
7 c 179 (Execution of Deeds).

1.09   After the passing of the Act of 1593 there were no
further changes for nearly 100 years. During that interval the
Acts of 1555, 1579 and 1593 were irregularly enforced by the
courts. The two Acts which laid the foundation of modern
practice were the Subscription of Deeds Act 1681 (c 5) and the
Deeds Act 1696 (c 15). These Acts were passed during the
reigns of Charles II and William III respectively. It is perhaps a
tribute to the Scottish legislators of the seventeenth century

that the provisions of these Acts remained basically unaltered until 1874. The Act of 1681 disposed of the difficulty that although previous statutes had provided for witnesses, they had not stated that the witnesses must sign and this made it easy for them to deny the fact of witnessing altogether.

'That only subscribing Witnesses, in writes to be subscribed by any partie hereafter shall be probative and not the witnesses insert not Subscribing; And that all such writes to be subscribed hereafter, wherein the Writer and witnesses are not designed, shall be null, And are not supplyable by condescending upon the Writer, or the designation of the Writer and Witnesses.'

This part of the Act uses the term 'probative' for the first time and also emphasises another important facet of a probative deed, namely that the statutory solemnities of execution must be apparent from the writ itself and cannot be supplied by 'condescending' or extrinsic evidence. The Act of 1681 went on to provide:

'That no witnes shall subscribe as witnes to any parties subscription, unless he then know that party, and saw him subscribe, or saw, or heard him give Warrand to a Nottar or Nottars to subscribe for him; And in evidence thereof, touch the Nottars pen, or that the party did, at the time of the witnesses subscribing, acknowledge his subscription. Otherways, the saids witnesses shall be repute and punished as accessorie to forgerie. And being Writting is now so ordinary, His Majesty with consent foresaid Doeth enact and Declare that no witnesses But subscribing witnesses shall be probative.'

Presumably legal secretaries were less liable to sign as witnesses at the behest of their employers in 1681 without having seen the granter sign, given the criminal sanction in the Act. After 1681 the statutory solemnities were:
(1) the witnesses must sign;
(2) the writer of the deed must be named and designed in the body of the deed;
(3) the witnesses must be designed in the body of the deed;
(4) neither the name and designation of the writer nor the designation of the witnesses could be supplied by a separate proof;
(5) the witnesses must know the granter;

(6) the witnesses must see the granter sign or hear him or her acknowledge his or her subscription at the time when they, the witnesses, signed;

(7) where a notary signed the witnesses must see or hear the granter give warrant to the notary and in evidence touch the notary's pen.

1.10 The Act of 1696 dealt with deeds which were written bookwise. Up to this time deeds were written on a single sheet of parchment or paper or a roll of such sheets battered (ie fastened or pasted) together. Such rolls were subscribed at the end and when they were battered together they were side-scribed across the joinings of the sheets. The Act of 1696, in what must have been a great technological leap forward, noted the commercial problem of the time by stating:

'Our Soveraign Lord understanding the great trouble and inconveniencey the leidges are put to in finding out the clauses and passages in long Contracts Decreits Dispositions Extracts Transumpts and other securities consisting of many sheets battered together . . . Doth for remeid thereof . . . ordain that it shall be free hereafter for any person . . . to choose . . . to have them written by way of book in Leafs of Paper.'

Thereafter the Act went on to provide safeguards against the possible frauds which this innovation might make more likely by ordaining that:

'Every page be marked by the number first, second etc. and Signed as the margines were before and that the end of the last page make mention how many pages are therin contained, in which page only witnesses are to signe, in writts and Securities where witnesses are required by law.'

1.11 The long-standing statutory solemnities set out in the seventeenth century were eventually whittled down. The Form of Deeds Act 1856 (c 89) abolished the numbering of each page. The Conveyancing (Scotland) Act 1874 abolished the necessity of naming the writer of the deed and specifying the number of pages[1]. That Act also provided that witnesses need not be named and designed in the body of the deed or in the testing clause, provided that their designations or descriptions were added after their signatures; such designations could be added at any time before the deed was recorded in any register for preservation or was founded on in court. Further, the designations did not require to be written by the witnesses themselves but could be added by someone else[1]. The statutory rules in relation to the solemnities of execution remained much as they were from 1874 until 1970, when a further and important simplification was made[2]. From 29 November 1970 any deed other than a will or testamentary writing required only to be subscribed or, where appropriate, sealed on the last page and on the last pages of any inventory, schedule, plan or document annexed. Wills and testamentary writings, however, still required subscription on each page. The requirements for witnessing remained the same.

1 Conveyancing (Scotland) Act 1874, s 38.
2 Conveyancing and Feudal Reform (Scotland) Act 1970, s 44.

The pressure for change

1.12 It is the authors' view that the authentication statutes and the more modern statutes up to 1970 relating to the execution of deeds had two main objectives:
(1) to prevent forgery and fraud; and
(2) to provide a special type of deed which proved its own authenticity.
In this respect the authentication statutes were by and large successful. Even at the time when the changes wrought by the Conveyancing and Feudal Reform (Scotland) Act 1970 were being considered there was a body of opinion which felt that it was risky to allow deeds (other than wills or testamentary writings) to be signed only on the last page. There was nothing to stop an unscrupulous person unstitching a deed, removing a page and inserting a completely different page, which the granter of the deed had never seen. However, these fears have proved largely groundless. In any event, there are two practical truths which have to be faced in contemplating any rules relating to the execution of deeds. First, the granters of deeds very seldom read over the whole contents of the deeds before signing. Secondly, if a person has decided to

commit forgery or fraud he or she will find a way of doing so, irrespective of any authentication statute.

1.13 The law relating to the execution of deeds and attestation by witnesses goes back a long time. Section 39 of the Conveyancing (Scotland) Act 1874 provided a cure for informalities of execution but despite this a mistake in execution could result in the complete nullity of the deed. For this reason there has always been pressure to relax the statutory solemnities. No matter what statutory solemnities exist there will always be pressure to relax them and conversely there will always be pressure to retain solemnities for the prevention of fraud. It is at all times a question of trying to strike the right balance between the certainty of deeds and the freedom of parties to contract in the manner of their own choosing. There has always been, and always will be, a tension between these two objectives. In 1947 Lord President Cooper criticised the requirements laid down by the authentication statutes in trenchant terms:

'This reclaiming motion discloses a sharp conflict between the technical rule of our common law and the plain equities of the case. The ratio of the rule has often been explained in much the same terms, and I take as its best statement the familiar passage in Erskine (III, 2, 2) that "in the transmission of heritage, which is justly accounted of the greatest importance to society, parties are not to be caught by rash expressions, but continue free till they have discovered their deliberate and final resolution concerning it by writing". Writing has been interpreted as meaning writing probative of both parties to any contract, thus carrying the rule further than in the Statute of Frauds or any other provision of which I am aware. It is useless to disguise that, the further we recede from the far distant days when land was the substance of the private wealth of the community, the more clearly does this rule stand revealed as a fossil relic of feudalism, explicable, if confined within the field of strict conveyancing, but completely out of touch with realities when it intrudes into the field of mutual contract. It is emphatically not a rule for benignant interpretation or extended application'[1].

1 *McGinn v Shearer* 1947 SC 334 at 344.

1.14 The view of the Scottish Law Commission was that it was inappropriate to regulate the execution of deeds and documents with reference to Acts of Parliament which go back to the sixteenth century. The Scottish Law Commission looked at constitution and proof of voluntary obligations and issued a consultative memorandum in 1977[1]. As a result of the first consultation process a second consultative memorandum was issued in 1985[2]. As a result of both consultative processes, the Scottish Law Commission issued a report on the requirements of writing in 1988[3]. The report was presented to the Lord Advocate and there was an attempt to enact legislation, but this failed for procedural reasons. The report languished until 1995 when its recommendations were enacted in the Requirements of Writing (Scotland) Act 1995. The report contained 45 recommendations. The main proposals were:

(1) In general any rule requiring a contract to be constituted by formal (ie attested or holograph) writing should be abolished.

(2) A written document would still be required for the constitution of any contract or voluntary obligation for the creation, transfer, variation or extinction of an interest in land, for the constitution of a gratuitous obligation except when undertaken in the course of business, for the constitution of a trust whereby a person declares himself or herself the sole trustee of his or her own property or any property which he or she might acquire, and for the creation, transfer or extinction of an interest in land and the making of a testamentary settlement.

(3) While writing would still be required in relation to contracts or obligations for the creation, transfer, variation or extinction of interests in land the writing would not require to be in probative form unless the deed in question was to be recorded in the Register of Sasines, Books of Council and Session or Sheriff Court books, in which case attestation by one witness would be necessary. The Land Register was not mentioned in this context because the Keeper already had an overall discretion as to what documents are accepted for the purposes of land registration[4].

(4) Privileged documents, including holograph writings, writings adopted as holograph and writings *in re mercatoria*, would no longer have any particular status.

(5) There should be new rules in relation to alterations to deeds.

(6) The concept of probativity as an evidential matter should be retained, but new attestation requirements less onerous than under the authentication statutes should be set out.

(7) The concepts of *rei interventus* and homologation would be abolished and replaced by a new statutory concept of personal bar.

(8) In a case where a document did not fulfil the new requirements for probativity it would still be possible to apply to the court to have it certified as probative, which application could be supported by affidavit evidence as to the actual subscription of the deed.

(9) There should be new rules relating to the execution of deeds by limited companies and corporate bodies.

1 Consultative memorandum no 39, Constitution and Proof of Voluntary Obligations: Formalities of Constitution and Restrictions on Proof.
2 Consultative memorandum no 66, Constitution and Proof of Voluntary Obligations and the Authentication of Writings.
3 Scot Law Com no 112.
4 Land Registration (Scotland) Act 1979, s 4(1).

Criticisms of the proposals

1.15 By and large the main proposals were welcomed in relation to the reduction in the number of witnesses. However, there was concern over the status of missives in relation to the new proposals. A large body of opinion felt that missives were an important enough contract to require probative writing. While no one wished to see missives attested as such, it was felt by many that the status of holograph writings should have been retained and that missives should have required holograph writing as at the present time. These criticisms were rejected by the Scottish Law Commission mainly on the ground that the words 'adopted as holograph' were unintelligible to lay people. An alternative proposal that the words 'intended to be binding' be substituted for the words 'adopted as holograph' was also rejected. It may be that the legal profession will take the view that it is important for missives to be probative in the evidential sense if nothing else and that they will choose to have them signed by the parties and attested by a single witness, or alternatively signed by solicitors as before and attested by a single witness[1].

1 For a detailed discussion of the criticisms in relation to the abolition of holograph status see *Cusine and Rennie* paras 2.20, 2.21.

1.16 Although the 1995 Act may be seen by many as a radical overhaul of the law relating to the execution of deeds, it still continues the notion of a deed which is probative by subscription and attestation, with the alternative of notarial execution where a party is blind or unable to write. These were the three main innovations of the Subscription of Deeds Act 1540. The 1995 Act hopes to provide a framework for the execution of deeds which will be safe and practical in a modern age. The authors hope, however, that they may be allowed to shed two tears at the final repeal of the Acts of 1540, 1579, 1681 and 1696. It is a little sad to see these Acts of the Scottish Parliament, which have served the law and commerce so well, pass away almost unnoticed as a consequential repeal in Schedule 5 to the Requirements of Writing (Scotland) Act 1995 – a United Kingdom statute at that!

The 1995 Act received the Royal Assent on 1 May 1995 and comes into force on 1 August 1995.

CHAPTER 2

The law prior to 1995

Introduction

2.01 Even after the Requirements of Writing (Scotland) Act 1995, it will still be necessary to have a knowledge of the previous law, which itself has changed from time to time. A knowledge of the previous law is clearly of importance in examination of title and we hope that this chapter, which sets out the main features, will prove to be a readily available first source or spot check. Further detail can be obtained from Halliday *Conveyancing Law and Practice in Scotland* [1]; McDonald's *Conveyancing Manual* [2] and the *Stair Memorial Encyclopaedia* [3].

It is worth observing at the outset that the 1995 Act does not greatly affect subscription by natural persons [4] whether as granters (personally) or as authorised officials, eg on behalf of a company, attorneys, etc or as witnesses. It also does not affect the question of who may act as witnesses, when the witnessing should take place, nor the form and status of testing clauses.

The foundation of the law both before and after the 1995 Act is the Subscription of Deeds Acts 1540–1681. The 1681 Act followed upon previous attempts to lay down a set of coherent rules. This Act and subsequent legislation is, of course, concerned only with formal validity, rather than essential validity, and one has to look behind the execution of deeds to ascertain, for example, whether the parties had contractual capacity, whether the document was signed under duress, whether the purposes of the transaction was illegal or contrary to public policy and whether the transaction was tainted by essential error or misrepresentation. What follows, however, is restricted to a consideration of formal, and not essential, validity.

---

1 Vol 1, Ch 3. For testamentary documents see A R Barr et al *Drafting Wills in Scotland* (1994) paras 2.31–2.58, 2.73–2.75.
2 (5th edn, 1993) Ch 1.

3 6 *Stair Memorial Encyclopaedia* paras 413–433.
4 There is a minor exception in relation to signature by mark; see para 3.12.

Acts 1540–1970

2.02 The Subscription of Deeds Act 1540 required subscription by the granter, and witnesses, and it went on to provide that if the granter could not sign, then a notary could act on his or her behalf. There were subsequent Acts in 1579, 1584 and 1593 but the Subscription of Deeds Act 1681, while making no change to the requirement that the granter had to subscribe on every page, went on to provide that:

(1) the witnesses must sign the deed;
(2) the witnesses must be named and designed;
(3) the witnesses must know the granter;
(4) the notary must see the granter sign or hear him or her acknowledge his or her signature at the time when they sign; and
(5) where a notary signs, the witnesses to that execution must see or hear the granter give authority to the notary.

None of these Acts indicated how many witnesses there had to be and convention has it that there are two. The Deeds Act 1696 required that where deeds were written bookwise, as they are today, the pages had to be numbered and the deed had to mention the number of pages. The requirement to number the pages was removed in 1874 and the requirement to mention the number of pages in the testing clause was abolished in 1856. The Conveyancing (Scotland) Act 1874 permitted the designation of witnesses to be added at any time prior to to the deed being registered in any public register for preservation or founded upon in court.

The 1970 Act

2.03 A major change took place in 1970 with the passing of the Conveyancing and Feudal Reform (Scotland) Act 1970 which, as from 29 November 1970, dropped the requirement for subscription on every page. With the exception of testamentary documents, the requirement was (and still is) that the deed should be signed on the last page. The 1970 Act went on to provide that inventories, schedules, plans or other annexations should be signed on the last page only[1].

Prior to the coming into force of the 1995 Act, the requirements were:

(1) that the document had to be subscribed by the granter personally or by someone on his or her behalf on the last page;

(2) any plan, inventory, schedule or other annexation had to be signed on the last page also;

(3) a testamentary document had to be signed on every page;

(4) the granter had to sign in the presence of or acknowledge his or her signature to at least two competent witnesses;

(5) the witnesses had to subscribe on the last page only;

(6) the witnesses had to be designed in the deed.

While this would normally be in the testing clause, the designations could appear after the witnesses' signatures, and need not be in the witnesses' handwriting.

1 Section 44.

Inessentials

2.04 It has never been essential but it is common to find

(1) a statement of the number of pages;

(2) the date and place of signature, either or both of which may assist anyone seeking to uphold or deny the validity of the deed. The date is also useful for stamp duty purposes where there may be a requirement that a deed is stamped within 30 days of its execution;

(3) the addition of the word 'witness' added after a witness's signature to establish that the witness is signing in that capacity and not as a granter.

We now go on to consider in some more detail the various requirements outlined above.

Subscription of the granter

2.05 Only the sovereign may superscribe but frequently also subscribes. All other granters must, however, subscribe. Anything which appears after the subscription is disregarded[1].

Where a deed consists of a single sheet folded to make several pages, there must be sufficient connection between the pages and the subscriptions of the granter[2].

1 *Taylor's Executrices v Thom* 1914 SC 79; *M'Lay v Farrell* 1950 SC 149; *Ayrshire Hospice, Petitioners* 1993 SLT (Sh Ct) 75.
2 *Baird's Trustees v Baird* 1955 SC 286; *Ferguson, Petitioner* 1959 SC 56; *Bogie's Executors v Bogie* 1953 SLT (Sh Ct) 32.

Mode of signature
MEN, MARRIED WOMEN, PEERS

2.06 Men and married women sign their surname in full, prefixed by any of the following: their forenames in full, or recognised contractions of one or more of these names, or the initials of these names, or any combination of these. Thus, Alexander James Walker may sign 'Alexander James Walker' or 'Alexander J Walker' or 'A James Walker' or 'Alex J Walker' or 'AJ Walker'. If all the forenames used in the deed are not represented in the signature, then the testing clause should note the discrepancy and contain, for example, the phrases 'subscribing Alex Walker' or 'subscribing his usual signature Alex Walker'. Married women frequently use their husband's surname prefaced by their own forenames or initials or recognised contractions. They may, however, use their maiden surname instead of their married surname[1]. While it is strictly incorrect for a married woman to sign both her maiden surname and her married surname, or any contraction of both, it has been held that this does not render the subscription invalid[2].

An exception to the rule that surnames alone do not suffice is that peers of the realm subscribe using only their titles. They normally use the highest title if they have more than one unless the deed relates to an inferior title[3]. Thus, the Duke of Argyll subscribes 'Argyll'. In *American Express v Royal Bank*[4], there was evidence that someone who was not a peer of the realm customarily signed his surname only and that was upheld. In the absence of that type of evidence, however, a surname alone does not suffice even if it is prefixed by 'Mr or Mrs' as the case may be[5]. However, a proper signature is not invalidated because it is prefixed with 'Mr' or 'Mrs' etc[6]. It follows also that a signature by initials is not sufficient. Unless there is a statutory provision authorising signature by initials or a mark, such a signature is invalid[7]. In some instances, however, a less formal form of execution has been permitted, for example a signature by a name eg 'Connie' or simply the word 'Mum'[8]. Each of these cases involved writings of a testamentary nature and extrinsic evidence was required to establish the identity of the testator, and the fact that the subscription was customary or not unusual in the circumstances. Although a signature need not be legible[9], it must, however, be complete[10].

It is essential that the subscription is a voluntary act of the granter and so while the granter's hand may be supported, while he or she signs[11], it must not be led by another or signed over traces made by another[12]. A signature by stamp or cyclostyle or other mechanical or artificial means is also theoretically invalid[13] but, in practice, such signatures are accepted, where the signatory is signing on behalf of a reputable body. For example, many signatures on behalf of insurance companies, banks and building societies may take this form and are unlikely to be challenged.

On the other hand, a signature which is written on an erasure is valid[14], as is a faint signature which has been gone over by the original signatory[15].

1 *Dunlop v Greenlees Trustees* (1863) 2 M 1.
2 *Grieve's Trustees v Japp's Trustees* 1917 1 SLT 70.
3 Lord Lyon King of Arms Act 1672.
4 1989 SLT 650.
5 *Allan and Crichton, Petitioners* 1933 SLT (Sh Ct) 2.
6 *Ferguson, Petitioner* 1959 SC 56.
7 *Gardner v Lucas* (1878) 5 R (HL) 105; see also M C Meston and D J Cusine 'Execution of deeds by a mark' (1993) 38 JLSS 270.
8 *Draper v Thomason* 1954 SC 136; *Rhodes v Peterson* 1972 SLT 198.
9 *Stirling Stuart v Stirling Crawfurd's Trustees* (1885) 12 R 610.
10 *Moncreiff v Monypenny* (1710) Mor 15936.
11 *Noble v Noble* (1875) 3 R 74.
12 *Moncreiff v Monypenny*, above (hand led); *Crosbie v Pickens* (1749) Mor 16814 (traces made by another).
13 *Stirling Stuart v Stirling Crawfurd's Trustees* (1885) 12 R 610.
14 *Brown v Duncan* (1888) 15 R 511.
15 *Stirling Stuart*, above.

PARTNERSHIPS

2.07 In Scotland, deeds which require to be attested are executed by all of the partners adhibiting their signatures and it is common for the partnership name to be adhibited by one of the partners. These signatures have to be witnessed. A distinction has to be drawn, however, between these deeds and documents which are executed in the ordinary course of business of the firm. In such matters, every partner is an agent of both the firm and the other partners with authority to bind the firm, and accordingly the signature of the partner or the signature of the firm's name is enough[1]. Thus, it is in the ordinary course of business of solicitors to sign missives 'adopted as holograph' with either the partner's name or the firm's name thereunder. It should be noted, however, that only a partner may sign, and accordingly the manager of a branch office of a firm of estate agents who was not a partner could not competently sign on behalf of the firm[2].

1 Partnership Act 1890, s 5.
2 *Littlejohn v MacKay* 1974 SLT (Sh Ct) 82; see, however, D J Cusine and J Pearson 'Who signs for the firm?: *Littlejohn v MacKay* revisited' (1991) 36 JLSS 73.

LOCAL AUTHORITIES

2.08 Prior to 1973, local authorities consisted of town and county councils, and under the Local Government (Scotland) Act 1947 deeds had to be sealed with the common seal and subscribed by two members of the council and the clerk. These signatures did not, however, have to be witnessed. With the reorganisation of local government in 1973, district, regional and island councils were introduced, and in terms of the Local Government (Scotland) Act 1973, s 194 a deed may be executed with the common seal of the local authority and subscribed by two members and a proper officer. Witnesses are not required to these signatures. A proper officer for this purpose means any officer appointed for that purpose and it is normally the chief executive, or some other head of department. The Local Government (Scotland) Act 1994 did not alter this position, but changes are made by the 1995 Act[1].

1 See para 4.06.

BUILDING SOCIETIES

2.09 Under the Building Societies Act 1986, a building society must have a common seal and rules governing its use.

Accordingly reference should be made to the rules of the particular society in order to verify the mode of execution. Normally, however, the building society sends with the particulars of signing an excerpt from the rules indicating who is able to sign. The normal method for execution of formal deeds is by the seal, an authorised signatory and two witnesses.

COMPANIES

2.10 The requirements for the execution of deeds by companies has given rise to some confusion. Until 30 July 1990, the relevant provision was the Companies Act 1985, s 36(3) which replaced an earlier provision in the Companies Act 1948 which itself reflected provisions in earlier Acts. In terms of that legislation, a deed was validly executed by a company if
(1) it was executed in accordance with the provisions of the Act; or
(2) was sealed with the common seal and subscribed on behalf of the company by two directors or one director and the secretary.
The legislation provided that if method (2) was used witnesses were not required. There was, however, some confusion about whether witnesses were required if method (1) was used and the confusion can be seen in *Clydesdale Bank (Moore Place) Nominees Ltd v Snodgrass*[1]. On the basis of that case, there ought to be at least two signatures and the seal, and two of the judges thought that the signatures of the two directors, or the director and the secretary, were sufficient to witness the affixing of the seal. An attempt was made to alter the law by the Companies Act 1989, s 130, but that section itself had to be replaced by the Law Reform (Miscellaneous Provisions) (Scotland) Act 1990, s 72. On or after 31 July 1990, a document is validly executed by a company if it is subscribed on behalf of the company by two of the directors, or a director and the secretary, or two persons authorised to subscribe the document on behalf of the company, and these authorised persons include a director and the secretary. It is, however, no longer necessary for a company to have a seal and these methods are valid whether or not the subscription is witnessed[2]. Receivers, administrators, administrative receivers and liquidators all have authority to execute deeds on behalf of the company. The seal

may be used, but it is essential that there is the signature of the relevant person and that the signature is witnessed in the usual way. The provisions of the Companies Act 1985, s 36B apply only to the execution of deeds by the company.

1 1939 SC 805.
2 Companies Act 1985, s 36B.

Statutory bodies–corporate names

2.11 In considering deeds executed by bodies incorporated under statute, it is important to bear in mind that the body's name is as described in the certificate of incorporation or equivalent documentation, and that name should be used on all occasions. Thus, there is no such body known as 'The Halifax Building Society' but the 'Halifax Building Society' does exist and is the proper name of the building society.

In connection with companies, there have been occasions where the name of the company as the grantee, say in a disposition, differs from the name of the company in the subsequent deed where the company is the granter, and there have also been instances where the name of the company as granter in the body of the deed differs from what appears on the seal. If there is a disposition to the company under a different name from the name in which the company is incorporated, the deed is, subject to the provisions of s 27 of the Companies Act 1985, invalid. Likewise, although there may have been a valid conveyance to the company, because the company as grantee of the deed has been correctly named, if the company is wrongly named as granter in the subsequent deed, the company will not have divested itself of the property by the purported disposition. If the company has then been struck off, the company's property will have vested in the Crown as *bona vacantia* under the Companies Act 1985, s 654. In these circumstances a disposition may be obtainable by the Queen's and Lord Treasurer's Remembrancer in order to correct the situation.

As has been mentioned, however, there is a provision in s 27 of the Companies Act 1985 whereby certain contractions are recognised. These are 'Ltd' for 'Limited' and 'PLC' for 'Public Limited Company', and the Welsh equivalents. In terms of s 26 the word 'and' and '&' are to be regarded as the same. These are, however, the only deviations from the norm which are valid. Thus, the omission of 'and' or 'Co' or brackets, or other part of the incorporated name is, in the authors' opinion, invalid. We can only speculate that a court might regard the omission of a punctuation mark as *de minimis*.

Witnesses

2.12 The following persons cannot competently act as witnesses:
(1) persons under the age of 16, by virtue of the Age of Legal Capacity (Scotland) Act 1991;
(2) persons who are *non compos mentis*;
(3) persons who cannot write;
(4) persons who have signed the same deed as principals, because witnesses must be independent;
(5) persons who are blind, because they cannot see the granter subscribe. (They can, of course, hear him acknowledge his or her signature but cannot make the necessary link between the acknowledgment and the signature.)

It is, however, no objection that a witness is related to the granter, or has an interest in the deed, eg as a beneficiary[1], nor does it matter that a witness is appointed in the deed as a trustee[2]. However, for obvious reasons, it is best to avoid having witnesses who are other than truly independent. The witness must know the granter but all that is required is a reliable introduction[3]. That requirement excludes a witness who sees or hears a granter sign, but by accident or stealth. Although the witness needs to know the granter, there is no requirement for the witness to know the contents of the deed[4].

The style, place and method of signature for the witness is the same as is required for the granter, but witnesses normally sign opposite the granter's signature and need sign on the last page only. It is customary to add the word 'witness' after the name, but it is competent for someone else to do so. In terms of the Conveyancing (Scotland) Act 1874, s 38 the designation of witnesses after their signature may be added at any time, provided that it is done before the deed is registered for preservation or is founded upon in court.

1 *Simson v Simson* (1883) 10 R 1247.
2 *Mitchell v Miller* (1742) Mor 16900.
3 *Brock v Brock* 1908 SC 964.
4 *Ormistoun v Hamilton* (1708) Mor 16890.

Time of signature

2.13 The relevant statutes are silent on this particular matter but, in practice, witnesses should sign immediately after the granter signs or immediately after hearing the granter acknowledge his or her signature. The leading case is *Walker v Whitwell*[1]. The House of Lords cast doubt on earlier decisions where there had been a significant interval between the signature of the granter and the witnessing. *Walker* is also authority for the proposition that the witness signs only if he or she has authority from the granter and that authority falls on the death of the granter, as in *Walker*, or in the case of insanity. The lack of a mandate also excludes someone who sees the granter sign by stealth or accident. In *MacDougall v MacDougall's Executors*[2] it was averred that a solicitor who had acted as a witness left the granter's presence, but on a landing outside the granter's room and within earshot explained that another witness would be required, and asked McL to act as a witness which he did. A proof before answer was allowed but the action was later abandoned. If this were permitted, it would be stretching the notion of acknowledgment by the granter of his or her signature, but the circumstances might be such that the granter would have been personally barred from denying that the witness had authority to act. The acts of subscribing and witnessing are intended to be parts of a single act of execution and as such should be performed *unico contextu*[3].

1 1916 SC (HL) 75.
2 1994 SLT 1178; see *Lindsay v Milne* 1995 SLT 487.
3 *Walker v Whitwell*, above; *Hynd's Trustee v Hynd's Trustees* 1955 SC (HL) 1.

Reduction of deeds because of defects in attestation

2.14 The onus of proving that a deed which is *ex facie* valid is nevertheless defectively executed is a heavy one and the onus of proof lies on the challenger[1]. It has been held that evidence from one witness that she had not seen the granter sign the deed was insufficient[2]. However, *prima facie* grounds for challenge may be excluded by personal bar, especially where it is the granter of the deed who is seeking to deny its validity, on the ground of defective attestation[3].

1 *McArthur v McArthur's Executors* 1931 SLT 463.
2 *Forrest v Low's Trustees* 1907 SC 1240.
3 For an example, see *Boyd v Shaw* 1927 SC 414.

Testing clauses

2.15 The purpose of the testing clause is to record the particulars of execution, but it also has a subsidiary function of mentioning alterations, interlineations or erasures which have been made prior to signature. It is clear that although the testing clause forms part of the deed, it cannot be used to alter or add to the terms of the deed itself. Any such purported alterations in the testing clause are disregarded[1]. The whole of the testing clause of the deed ought to appear above the granter's signatures and if part of the testing clause appears on the next page there is some doubt as to the validity of the deed[2].

1 *Smith v Chambers' Trustees* (1878) 5 R (HL) 151; *Blair v Assets Company* (1896) 23 R (HL) 36; cf *Gibson's Trustees v Lamb* 1931 SLT 22.
2 *Baird's Trustees v Baird* 1955 SC 286.

Time of completion of the testing clause

2.16 Although there are early cases in which there was a considerable delay in completing the testing clause, the best practice, in the light of *Walker v Whitwell*, is to ensure that the testing clause is completed as soon as possible after the execution by the various granters and the witnesses. The Conveyancing (Scotland) Act 1874, s 38 provides that the designation of the witnesses which need not appear in the testing clause may be added at any time (and not necessarily by the witnesses) prior to the deed being founded upon in court, or being registered for preservation.

Errors in the testing clause

2.17 If there is an error in a material part of the testing clause that may be fatal, but an error such as a name typewritten on an erasure may be disregarded if the information can be obtained from the signatures[1]. The testing clause can itself be corrected by restarting the testing clause after the words 'that is to say' following upon the error.

1 *M'Dougall v M'Dougall* (1875) 2 R 814.

Alterations in deeds: additions, deletions, erasures, interlineations

2.18 Prior to 1995 there was a presumption that alterations or additions to an attested deed were made after execution, and so if such a change had not been authenticated it would be treated as *pro non scripto*. If, of course, these changes are not material, the deed is not affected, but if they are material[1], and they usually are, the deed is null, or if they occurred in a part of the deed which was severable, only that part is null[2].

1 *Boswell v Boswell* (1852) 14 D 378; *Reid v Kedder* (1840) 1 Robin 183, HL.
2 *Halliday* vol 1, para 3–24.

Erasures

2.19 If there has been an erasure and words have been completely obliterated, the courts assume that the words were important and accordingly the deed, or that part of the deed, does not receive effect. However, it may be that the context demonstrates that the words were not important or the information which has been erased can be supplied from another part of the deed[1].

1 *M'Dougall v M'Dougall* (1875) 2 R 814.

Material alterations

2.20 If any words to be added to the deed are material, the proper course is to insert them in the margin of the deed (linking them with their proper position in the text with an insertion (caret) mark) and have them plainly authenticated by having them side-scribed on either side. In practice, although this is not strictly speaking necessary, the alteration is also noted in the testing clause. An example is *Munro v Butler Johnstone*[1] where the word 'not' had been inserted in a clause, but because it was not authenticated the whole deed was ineffective. The important point, however, is that the alterations are authenticated in some way, but, as a general rule, the courts do not allow extrinsic evidence[2].

1 (1868) 7 M 250.
2 See *Reid v Kedder* (1840) 1 Robin 183, HL.

Minor alterations

2.21 If the alteration is minor it is sufficient to have it declared in the testing clause. Minor marginal additions ought to be clearly marked, in the sense that the place where they are to be inserted ought to be clear.

Blanks

2.22 Blanks are dealt with both at common law and by statute. If a blank appears in a material part of the deed, the deed is ineffectual[1]. If, however, the blank appears in a part which is not material and that part can be separated from the rest of the deed, the part containing the blank is not regarded as probative, but the rest of the deed receives effect[2]. If a blank has been filled in after execution, but before the deed is founded upon, it is possibly probative if the words which have been filled in have been authenticated. If, however, there is no authentication, it is presumed that the words were filled after execution and without the consent of the granter, and hence are invalid[3].

1 *Ewen v Ewen's Trustees* (1830) 4 W & S 346, HL.
2 *Abernethy v Forbes* (1835) 13 S 263.
3 *Earl of Buchan v Scottish Widows Fund Society* (1857) 19 D 551, the opinion of Lord Justice-Clerk Hope.

2.23 The Blank Bonds and Trusts Act 1696 provided that a deed was to be treated as null if the grantee's name was not inserted either before the deed was signed or before it was delivered. If it was to be inserted before delivery, the insertion had to take place before the same witnesses to the original execution. If it was established that the name of the grantee was not inserted before execution, the onus of proving that it was inserted before delivery in the presence of the original witnesses rested on the person who maintained that the deed was valid[1].

The effect of the common law and statute law prior to 1 August 1995 on blanks is as follows:

(1) If the name of the grantee was blank when the deed was executed, it was null by virtue of the 1696 Act, at least as regards that particular grantee. If the name of the grantee was material, as it normally would be, the deed was not valid at common law.

(2) If in any attested deed a blank was left when it was executed, the deed was not probative *quoad* the part left blank. If, however, the space had subsequently been filled up, but without authentication and without it being noticed in the testing clause, the onus of establishing the insertion was made with the consent of the granter rested upon the person founding upon the deed.

(3) Only the part left blank was effected by the statutory or common law rules. The rules of the deed, if separable, would stand.

1 *Donaldson v Donaldson* (1749) Mor 9080.

Deeds partly printed

2.24 There are special statutory rules which apply here. Section 149 of the Titles to Land Consolidation (Scotland) Act 1868, as amended by the Conveyancing (Scotland) Act 1874, s 38 provided that if these deeds had a testing clause and the date appeared in it, they were as valid and effectual as if they had been wholly in writing. It was, however, the practice, but not necessary, to narrate in the testing clause that the deed was partly printed and partly typewritten.

Alterations in testamentary writings

2.25 Alterations in attested testamentary writings made before execution are treated in exactly the same way as alterations made to any other deed prior to execution. There are, however, special rules relating to alterations to testamentary writings which are made *post-execution*. The issue here is whether an alteration subsequently made should receive effect, but the test is not one of authentication but whether the alteration represents the testator's intentions. The leading case is *Pattison's Trustees v the University of Edinburgh*[1] and the four points are set out by Lord McLaren[2]. These are:

(1) If a will is found with the signature cancelled or with lines drawn through the dispositive clause or other essential clause then, if there is proof that this was done by the testator or on his instructions with the intention of revoking the will, it is held to be revoked.

(2) If a will is found with one or more legacy or particular provisions scored out, that does not raise any question about the revocation of the whole will, but only of the parts involved. These parts are held to be revoked if there is evidence that this was done by the testator or on his or her instructions.

(3) If a will is found with marginal additions or interlineations, even in the testator's own handwriting, they do not receive effect unless they are authenticated by the signature or initials of the testator.

(4) If a will is found with words scored out and others substituted, the cancellation is conditional on the substituted words taking effect. In other words if the substituted words are rejected because of lack of authentication, the deletion is also disregarded and the will takes effect in its original form.

An example of the operation of the rules can be seen in *Thomson's Trustees v Bowhill Baptist Church*[3]. In that case, on the death of the testator, a copy of her will was found and she had made a number of deletions or alterations on the copy. The original will was held by her solicitor. The surrounding circumstances were such as to convince the court that these alterations should be given effect to. The testatrix had cut out the residue clause with scissors explaining that she did not have enough money to fulfil the provisions of that clause[4].

1 (1886) 16 R 73.
2 (1886) 16 R 73 at 76–77.
3 1956 SC 217.
4 See also *Syme's Executors v Cherrie* 1986 SLT 161.

Defects in execution

2.26 In some cases a defect in execution can be of such a minor nature that it may be ignored. For example, in *Dickson's Trustees v Goodall*[1] the name of a witness was 'Davys' whereas in the testing clause it appeared as 'Davis'. The deed was upheld on the basis that the two names sounded the same, and the irregularity was so trivial that it could not cast any doubt on the validity of the deed. Prior to 1874 a trivial defect could be overlooked; anything more serious, however, rendered the deed null.

1 (1820) Hume 924.

Informality of execution

2.27 The 1874 Act, s 39 provided that

'no deed, instrument or writing subscribed by the grantor or maker thereof, and bearing to be attested by two witnesses subscribing . . . shall be deemed invalid or denied effect . . . because of any informality of execution, but the burden of proving that such deed, instrument or writing so attested was subscribed by the grantor or maker thereof and by the witnesses by whom such deed, instrument or writing bears to be attested, shall lie upon the party using or upholding the same.'

The Act provided that proof might be lead in any action or proceedings upon which the deed was founded, or alternatively by petition to the Court of Session or sheriff court. In *Bisset, Petitioner*[1] there was a will consisting of two sheets, only one of which was signed. The court held that this could be cured under s 39, but the onus was on the petitioner to prove that the signatures were those of the granter and the witnesses. Affidavit evidence was produced and the will was upheld.

Between 1874 and 1995 the position was therefore that defects fell into three categories:

(1) defects of such a minor or trivial nature that they could be disregarded without resort to s 39;
(2) defects so radical that the deed was beyond cure; and
(3) defects sufficiently material as not to be capable of being overlooked but yet capable of being cured under s 39.

The three categories are best illustrated by reference to reported cases.

1 1961 SLT (Sh Ct) 19.

Minor defects

2.28 *Veasey v Malcolm's Trustees*[1]. The testing clause was not completed until after the granter's death. The deed was executed prior to the passing of the 1874 Act, but nevertheless it was held to be a probative deed because the omission could be supplied.

Grieve's Trustees v Japp's Trustees[2]. One granter's name was 'Isabella Wilson or Moncur' but she subscribed the deed 'Isabella C Moncur'. Another granter was 'Joan Colville or Brown' who subscribed 'Joan C Brown'. A petition under s 39 was dismissed as unnecessary.

Brown v Duncan[3]. The signature which was admittedly authentic of the granter was superimposed upon an erasure. The deed was held valid because the holograph character of the signature was sufficient evidence of the approval of the granter.

1 (1875) 2 R 748.
2 1917 1 SLT 70.
3 (1888) 15 R 511.

Major defects

2.29 *Smyth v Smyth*[1]. The deed was signed by the granter and ostensibly also by two witnesses. However, the 'witnesses' neither saw the granter sign nor heard him acknowledge his signature. It was held that the deed was invalid.

Moncreiff v Lawrie[2]. One of the witnesses to a minute of enactment in a public roup did not sign the minute and the deed was held to be invalid.

Walker v Whitwell[3]. One of the witnesses did not sign until after the granter's death and the deed was held to be invalid.

Irvine v McHardy[4]. This was a notarial execution in which the notary did not sign the docket as required by the 1874 (now the 1924) Act, and this was held to be invalid.

Baird's Trustees v Baird[5]. A will was written on a single sheet on both sides but with no carrying-forward word on the first page. The sheet was signed on both sides by the granter but witnessed only on the reverse side which was blank. It was held that since the form was on only one sheet the Deeds Act 1696 (which allowed deeds to be written bookwise and signed and witnessed on only the last page) did not apply. The attested signature on the back and blank side with no catchword was not a signature within the meaning of the 1540 and 1681 Acts and so the deed was invalid.

1 (1876) 3 R 573.
2 (1896) 23 R 577.
3 1916 SC (HL) 75.
4 (1892) 19 R 458.
5 1955 SC 286.

Defects curable under s 39

2.30 *McLaren v Menzies*[1]. In this case a deed consisted of two sheets, one stitched within the other to form eight pages. The granter signed on the fifth page followed by a docket which finished on the sixth page, which contained the signatures of three witnesses. There was a failure to sign every page, which was a requirement prior to 1970, and the deed was held to be curable.

Thomson's Trustees v Easson[2]. There was an omission to design the witnesses either in the deed or following their signatures. This was a case in which it was no longer competent to add the designations under s 38 because the deed had been founded upon in court, but nevertheless the defect was curable under s 39.

Richardson's Trustees[3]. The witness subscribed 'Roberton' but was named as 'Robertson' in the testing clause, and this was held to be a curable defect.

Bogie's Executors[4]. A will was written on two separate sheets, the second of which contained only part of the testing clause.

The document was signed on the second sheet only, but that was held to be curable, because there was some link between the words in the deed and the subscription.

Ferguson, Petitioner[5]. A will consisting of a printed form comprised a single sheet folded to make four pages. The substance of the will was on page 1 and the will was signed on page 1. There was a docket which started on page 1 and continued to page 3, but the document was witnessed on page 3 only. It was held that this was curable.

Elliot's Executors[6]. Unauthenticated alterations in a will with no declaration in the testing clause nor designation of witnesses were held to be curable. The undernoted cases provide further examples of curable defects[7]. Although s 39 disappears, the new Act introduces a similar provision[8].

1 (1876) 3 R 1151.
2 (1878) 6 R 141.
3 (1891) 18 R 1131.
4 1953 SLT (Sh Ct) 32.
5 1959 SC 56.
6 1939 SLT 69.
7 *Brown* (1883) 11 R 400; *Shiell* 1936 SLT 317; *Bisset, Petitioner* 1961 SLT (Sh Ct) 19; *McNeill v McNeill* 1973 SLT (Sh Ct) 16.
8 See para 3.25.

Notarial execution

2.31 Notarial execution was introduced by the Subscription of Deeds Act 1540 and further refinements were introduced by the Subscription of Deeds Acts of 1579 and 1681 and the Conveyancing (Scotland) Act 1874. The provision in the 1874 Act was replaced by the Conveyancing (Scotland) Act 1924, s 18. We shall look in detail at the requirements:

Who may use the procedure? The 1924 Act, s 18(1) provides that notarial execution is available to 'any person who, from any cause whether permanent or temporary' is blind or is unable to write. It is clear from the Schedules to the 1874 and 1924 Acts that the granter must declare to the notary that he or she has a disability. (It is not necessary that the person should have a disability, and any deed which is executed by a notary on behalf of someone who is truly able to write is nevertheless valid[1]. Another point is that the Acts do not say that notarial execution is the only possibility. For example, a blind person may sign a deed himself.[2])

Who may act? A solicitor, notary or justice of the peace and, in limited cases relating only to testamentary writings, ministers. A solicitor does not need to have a practising certificate[3], and a person acting as a clerk who is a qualified solicitor can act[4]. So far as ministers are concerned, the 1924 Act refers to ministers or assistant ministers within their own parishes but the Church of Scotland (Property and Endowments) Amendment Act 1933, s 13 provided that the power conferred in the 1924 Act was to be vested in the holder of any charge in the Church of Scotland.

The person acting must not have any disqualifying interest in the deed. If the person does have a disqualifying interest, the whole deed which has been notarially executed is invalid. This requirement has been strictly applied by the courts. A disqualifying interest may take a variety of forms, for example:

(a) a direct interest in the sense of being a beneficiary under a deed, or being a party to it. In *Lang v Lang's Trustees*[5], there was an antenuptial marriage contract between a man and a woman who was unable to write, and so the deed was signed by her husband's solicitor as notary. The husband attempted to set aside the contract arguing that the notary was not independent (there being a conflict of interest). Although the court held that there had been homologation, it is clear from the opinions that the deed would otherwise have been regarded as invalid.

(b) In *Newstead v Dansken*[6] where the notary was named as a solicitor to a trust in a document setting up the trust, with a power to charge fees, the deed was invalid. The notary in his capacity as solicitor to the trust would benefit from the fees charged.

(c) In *Ferrie v Ferrie's Trustees*[7] where the notary was named as one of the trustees in a deed notarially executed by him, but had no beneficial interest under the deed, it was nevertheless held to be invalid.

The office of trustee is gratuitous unless special power is given to make a charge. In *Ferrie v Ferrie's Trustees* there was power to appoint one of the trustees as law agent and to make a charge, and accordingly the notary might have benefitted. In *Finlay v Finlay's Trustees*[8] a partner of the notary was appointed as one of the trustees under a will by Dr Finlay. There was the usual power in the trustees to appoint one of their number to act as a solicitor and to charge professional fees. It was held that the notary would share in the fees if the partner acted and accordingly that person was barred from acting as notary, and the deed was invalid. In *Gorrie's Trustees v Stiven's Executrix*[9] the circumstances were identical, but the notary's explanation was that he had acted in circumstances of particular urgency owing to the illness of the granter. Nevertheless the result was the same and the court chose to disregard remarks in *Ferrie* about serious illness in a remote area as justifying a notarial execution. The strictest application of the rule can be seen in *Crawford's Trustees v Glasgow Royal Infirmary*[10]. A will was prepared by the testatrix and personally signed by her. In the will, one of the named trustees was a partner in a law firm and the will contained the usual clauses about appointing one of the trustees to act as a solicitor and to charge the usual professional remuneration. Later, because the testatrix was unable to write, she instructed a codicil and another partner in the firm executed the deed notarially for her. The codicil did not contain anything which could be construed as conferring a benefit on the notary. However, the court took the view that the codicil was invalid in that it had to be treated as *unum quid* with the will, and as the notary might share the fees under the will the codicil was invalid.

It does not follow that any connection, however remote, debars a notary. If an employee executes a deed notarially but has no other interest in the deed, that does not have the effect of rendering the deed invalid[11]. In *McIldowie v Muller*[12], there was no clause in the will allowing a solicitor who acted as law agent to charge fees. The will was executed notarially by a partner of the solicitor, but it was held that the notary did not have a disqualifying interest.

1 *Veitch v Horsburgh* (1637) Mor 16834.
2 *Duff v Earl of Fife* (1823) 1 Sh App 498.
3 *Stephen v Scott* 1927 SC 85.
4 *Hynd's Trustee v Hynd's Trustees* 1955 SC (HL) 1.
5 (1889) 16 R 590.
6 1918 1 SLT 136.
7 (1863) 1 M 291.
8 1948 SC 16.
9 1952 SC 1.
10 1955 SC 367.

11 *Hynd's Trustee v Hynd's Trustees* 1955 SC (HL) 1; *Aitken* 1965 SLT (Sh Ct) 15.
12 1979 SC 271.

Procedure

2.32 The procedure which must be carried out *unico contextu*[1] is as follows:

(1) the granter, the notary and the witnesses must assemble together;

(2) the deed has to be read over verbatim to the granter (but this is no longer required under the 1995 Act);

(3) the granter must declare that he or she is blind or otherwise incapacitated and give his or her authority to the notary. The authority need not be verbal but there must be something which the witnesses can see or hear which indicates consent;

(4) the notary appends a docket in the form set out in Schedule 1 to the 1924 Act and the docket must be in the notary's handwriting;

(5) the notary must sign on the last page below the docket, or in the case of a will on every page, just as the granter would; and

(6) the witnesses must sign immediately after the notary on the last page. The testing clause is in normal form as if the granter had signed himself or herself.

1 *Hynd's Trustee v Hynd's Trustees* 1955 SC (HL) 1.

Informalities and notarial execution

2.33 Although the 1874 Act, s 39 is available for any informality in notarial execution, it is difficult to envisage what informality of execution would be regarded as curable, given the strict approach which the courts have taken in this matter.

Privileged writings

2.34 Prior to the 1995 Act, there were certain categories to which the law accorded the same status as attested deeds even though they were not executed in accordance with the statutory solemnities. These were known as 'privileged writings' and within that category were holograph writings, those which were adopted as holograph, certain foreign deeds, writings *in re mercatoria* and writings privileged by statute. The status of privileged writings is abolished by the 1995 Act[1].

1 See para 3.38.

Holograph writings

2.35 A document which was completely in the handwriting of the granter would have received effect notwithstanding that the granter's signature was not witnessed. Deeds which were wholly in pencil or partly in ink and partly in pencil have been upheld[1]. Furthermore, a deed which purported to be witnessed, but where the witnessing was defective, would have been upheld as a valid holograph writ if it was in the granter's handwriting and signed by him[2].

There were, however, three important qualifications:

(1) The holograph writing had to be subscribed[3] but in the case of testamentary writings subscription by initials would have sufficed[4]. A deed can be holograph of only one party, and accordingly others would have had to have their signatures witnessed or have adopted the deed as holograph[5].

(2) Although the deed was privileged it was not self-proving and accordingly if a holograph writ was to be founded upon in court it would have been necessary to set up the deed by evidence of the granter's handwriting and the signature. In the case of the holograph writing which was to be used to obtain confirmation, the Succession (Scotland) Act 1964, s 21 provided that two affidavits are required as to the authenticity of the writing and the signature.

(3) A holograph document did not prove its own date except in the case of wills and acknowledgments of intimation of assignations[6].

1 *Tait's Trustees v Chiene* 1911 SC 743; *Manson v Edinburgh Royal Institution* 1948 SLT 196.
2 *Lorimer's Executors v Hird* 1959 SLT (Notes) 8.
3 *Taylor's Executrices v Thom* 1914 SC 79.

4 *Lowrie's Judicial Factor v McMillan* 1972 SC 105.
5 *Millar v Farquharson* (1835) 13 S 838.
6 Conveyancing (Scotland) Act 1874, s 40 (testamentary writings); *Gray v Earl of Selkirk* (1709) Robert 1 (assignation).

Alterations to holograph writings

2.36 Where the alterations are made to an *inter vivos* deed there is no presumption that these were made before delivery. Accordingly, such alterations require authentication in the same way as attested deeds. So far as testamentary writings are concerned the relevant question is whether these represent the granter's final intentions. If the amendments are in the granter's handwriting that of itself indicates that they were made with his or her consent[1]. In a special case, effect was given to unauthenticated deletions[2].

1 *Robertson v Ogilvie's Trustees* (1844) 7 D 236.
2 *Milne's Executor v Waugh* 1913 SC 203.

Writings partly holograph

2.37 These documents are frequently encountered as testamentary documents and two questions had to be asked: (1) whether in a particular case the words which were holograph contained in themselves all the essential parts of the deed and (2) what regard, if any, had to be given to the parts which were not holograph. The deed had to be looked at as a whole to ascertain its sense and if the holograph parts contained the minimum essentials of a valid will then the whole document was regarded as holograph and construed in accordance with its terms[1].

1 *Bridgeford's Executor v Bridgeford* 1948 SC 416; *Gillies v Glasgow Royal Infirmary* 1960 SC 430; and *Tucker v Canch's Trustee* 1953 SC 270.

Writings adopted as holograph in the document itself

2.38 A deed was regarded as being holograph if the granter wrote the words 'adopted as holograph' or their equivalent. The words were normally written above the signature of the granter. It was important that any granter of a document who was adopting a document as holograph should know what these words meant[1]. Other words such as 'accepted as holograph' would do and in a special case the words 'accepted as holograph', which should have been in the handwriting of the granter, were also typewritten. There was, however, evidence that the whole deed had been typed by the granter and that the granter had a physical disability as a result of which he always used a typewriter, and so the deed was upheld[2]. The requirements were that (1) the party using these words had to know that by using them he or she would be irrevocably bound; (2) the words normally had to precede the signature; and (3) the words normally had to be in the granter's handwriting.

1 *Harvey v Smith* (1904) 6 F 511; cf *Maclaine v Murphy* 1958 SLT (Sh Ct) 49.
2 *M'Beath's Trustees v M'Beath* 1935 SC 471; cf *Chisholm v Chisholm* 1949 SC 434.

Writings adopted by a separate deed

2.39 Here we are concerned with writings which are themselves informal, being neither attested nor holograph or even defective as to form, but which are rendered effective by being adopted in a separate deed which is valid. The adoption could be in advance or in arrears. The most common example of this is seen in wills or other unilateral deeds. For example, in *Waterson's Trustees v St Giles Boys' Club*[1], 'any informal writing under my hand' was held insufficient to cover an unsubscribed holograph writing. Before an informal writing can be adopted in this way four conditions must be satisfied:
(1) the deed or writing by which the imperfect writing is adopted must itself be validly executed or otherwise entitled to receive effect;
(2) the imperfect writing adopted must be unmistakably identified by the adopting deed or writing;
(3) the terms of the adopting document must make it clear that the writing which is being adopted is to be treated as expressing the subsisting wishes of the granter; and
(4) whichever document is later in date must be subscribed by the granter unless in the case of the imperfect document being later in date, the adopting document has dispensed with subscription of it.
In *Macrorie's Executors v McLaren*[2] the initial trust disposition gave the trustees power to give effect to 'all legacies and others

which may be contained in any future writings subscribed by me however otherwise informal the same may be'. It was held that that did not cover an unsigned codicil. The 1995 Act does not make any changes here. The courts may be reluctant to give effect to an unsigned document, unless there is a clear direction by the testator to that effect and, in practice, such directions are best avoided, because otherwise there could be confusion about whether something was intended as an *aide memoire*, or as the final wishes of the deceased.

1 1943 SC 369; *McGinn v Shearer* 1947 SC 334.
2 1982 SLT 295.

Writings in re mercatoria

2.40 Prior to 1995, there was no exhaustive definition of writings *in re mercatoria*, which were documents used in connection with commerce, such as cheques. These deeds did not need to be attested or holograph or adopted as holograph, but the privileges which they had have been abolished by the 1995 Act[1].

Certain deeds and writings are privileged by statute. For example a statute may provide that only one witness is required or that subscription may be without witnesses or that subscription may be by a mark.

1 See para 3.38; see *Halliday* vol 1, paras 3–72 ff.

Foreign deeds

2.41 Certain deeds which are executed outside Scotland may also be privileged and receive effect in Scotland even although they do not comply with our formalities. The two categories of deeds are non-testamentary and testamentary.

NON-TESTAMENTARY DEEDS

2.42 A deed relating to moveables receives effect in Scotland if the deed is executed in accordance with the law of the place of execution or, in the case of a contract, it conforms to the law of the place of performance of the contract. Thus, where there was a security over an insurance policy which was validly executed in accordance with English law, that was recognised in Scotland[1].

Inter vivos deeds relating to Scottish heritage must be validly executed in accordance with Scots law, which is the *lex loci situs*.

1 *Scottish Provident Institution v Cohen* (1886) 16 R 112.

TESTAMENTARY WRITINGS

2.43 Prior to 1 January 1964, a distinction was drawn between moveable estate and heritable estate. In the case of *moveable* estate, the documents were valid if executed in accordance with the law of the place of execution[1]. However, any will or testamentary document relating to *heritable* estate had to (1) disclose an intention to carry heritage and (2) be executed in the manner required or permitted by the law of Scotland in the case of a will relating to moveable property.

1 *Purvis's Trustees v Purvis's Executors* (1861) 23 D 812.

Deaths on or after 1 January 1964

2.44 The Wills Act 1963 deals with both heritable and moveable estate. A will is regarded as properly executed if its execution conforms to the internal law in force in:

(1) the territory where it was executed; or
(2) the territory where at the time of its execution, or of the testator's death, the testator was domiciled or had his or her habitual residence; or
(3) a state of which, at either of those times, he or she was a national[1].

A will is also regarded as properly executed so far as heritage is concerned if its execution conforms to the law in force in the territory where the property is situated. The Act contains other provisions of importance. For example, a will which revokes another will is valid if the revocation conforms, in terms of formal validity, with the law of the place of execution of the revoked will[2]. In relation to a will executed on board an aircraft or a ship, the Act provides that it is regarded as having been properly executed if the execution conforms to the internal law of the territory 'with which, having regard to its registration (if any) and any other relevant circumstances, the vessel or aircraft may be taken to have been most closely connected'[3]. 'Internal law' is defined as 'the law which would apply in a case where no question of the law in force in any other territory or state arose'[4].

1 Wills Act 1963, s 1.
2 Ibid, s 2(1)(c).
3 Ibid, s 2(1)(a).
4 Ibid, s 6(1).

CHAPTER 3

The law after 1995 – execution by individuals

The general principle

3.01 Previous law categorised certain undertakings as *obligationes literis*[1]. The basic principle of the Requirements of Writing (Scotland) Act 1995 is set out in s 1 where it is stated that writing is not required for the constitution of a contract, unilateral obligation or trust except as provided in the Act itself or in any other enactment. Accordingly, the main aim of the Act is to remove many of the rules relating to the formation of contract as opposed to the relaxation of existing formalities or restrictions. It is important to notice at the outset that in radically altering the existing law, the Act does not refer to probative or attested writing as such. It merely states that subject to certain exceptions, no writing of any sort is required for the formation of certain contracts. The Act received the Royal Assent on 1 May 1995 and comes into force on 1 August 1995.

1 See para 1.04.

The exceptions – contracts requiring writing

3.02 Immediately following the statement of general principle contained in s 1, it is provided in s 1(2) that a written document, properly subscribed, is required for certain contracts or deeds. Writing is required for:
(1) The constitution of a contract or unilateral obligation for the creation, transfer, variation or extinction of an interest in land (1995 Act, s 1(2)(a)(i))[1];
(2) The constitution of a gratuitous unilateral obligation except where undertaken in the course of business (s 1(2)(a)(ii));
(3) The constitution of a trust in which a person declares himself or herself to be sole trustee of his or her own property or any property which he or she may acquire (s 1(2)(a)(iii));

43

(4) The creation, transfer, variation or extinction of an interest in land other than by the operation of a court decree, enactment or rule of law (s 1(2)(b));

(5) The making of any will, testamentary trust disposition and settlement or codicil (s 1(2)(c)).

It is important to note that the requirement in relation to these exceptions is only that the deed should be in writing. There is no requirement that the deed should be witnessed in any way or otherwise authenticated. Where a document is required to be in writing, it is valid in respect of its execution if it has been subscribed by the granter or, if there is more than one granter, by each granter (s 2(1)). A document which constitutes a contract or unilateral obligation for the creation, transfer, variation or extinction of an interest in land, may be constituted or varied in more than one document, where there is an offer, a qualified acceptance and further documentation (s 2(2)). So far as the categories of contract or obligation which require writing are concerned these are self-explanatory. A contract or an obligation to create, transfer, vary or extinguish an interest in land[2] is a set of missives for these purposes. Land is still thought of as an important enough asset to require any contract or obligation relating to it to be in writing. A gratuitous unilateral obligation is a gratuitous promise which formerly required proof by writ or oath. It is easy to imagine the difficulties which could arise if one party attempted to prove that another party had given an oral promise to make a gift. A gratuitous promise made in the course of business need not be in writing. This may cause some difficulties, although most commercial dealings are in the nature of bilateral contracts as opposed to unilateral promises. The potential abuse which could arise in relation to oral declarations of trust by parties claiming to be their own trustee so as to put the property beyond the reach of creditors is obvious. The requirement that a document for the creation, transfer, variation or extinction of an interest in land, as opposed to a contract for these purposes, must also be in writing is merely a follow-through from the earlier principle. Feu charters, feu dispositions, dispositions, standard securities and discharges are all examples of documents which fall into this category. Wills and other testamentary writings also require to be in writing. This requirement is to avoid arguments as to what statement or statements made orally might be regarded as a testator's concluded intention. Although writing is still required in all of these cases, such writing no longer requires to be in probative or privileged writing in the sense of being signed and witnessed or holograph or adopted as holograph.

1 Interest in land is dealt with at para 3.10.
2 For the definition of an interest in land see para 3.10.

Personal bar

3.03 Under the previous law, where certain documents required to be in probative or holograph writing but had been constituted in improbative writing or by oral agreement, they could still receive effect if the agreement had been followed by actings of one party or the other, or both parties, which amounted to *rei interventus* or homologation[1]. Given the fact that the new Act does not require probative or holograph writing for the constitution of contracts, there clearly had to be a redefinition of the role of personal bar where the Act requires writing for the constitution of a contract, obligation or trust. Gone is the beauty of Bell's definition of *rei interventus* and homologation. The Act abolishes, or to use the words of the Act, 'replaces', the existing rules of law known as *rei interventus* and homologation (s 1(5)). In their place there is a new statutory form of personal bar. This applies where a contract, obligation or trust which ought to have been constituted in writing in terms of the Act has not been so constituted but where one of the parties to the contract or a creditor in the obligation or a beneficiary under the trust has acted or refrained from acting in reliance on the contract, obligation or trust with the knowledge and acquiescence of the other party to the contract, the debtor in the obligation or the truster. In these circumstances the contract, obligation or trust is not to be regarded as invalid and the party that has notice of the actings is not entitled to withdraw or repudiate merely on the ground that it has not been constituted in writing (s 1(3)). However, before the new statutory form of personal bar can apply, there are two requirements (s 1(4)). First, the party that seeks to uphold the contract, obligation or trust must have been affected to a material extent as a result of his or her actings or by reason of refraining from acting. Secondly, it must be shown that the party seeking to uphold the contract, obligation or trust would be adversely affected to a material extent if the other party were to withdraw. The statutory form of personal bar not only applies to the constitution of a contract, obligation or trust but also to any attempt to vary such a contract, obligation or trust (s 1(6)). The new statutory personal bar, however, does not apply to the other types of document which require writing, namely a document for the creation, transfer, variation or extinction of an interest in land or the making of any will or other testamentary writing. A close examination of this part of the Act shows how closely the new statutory personal bar follows the old doctrine of *rei interventus*. All the old familiar hurdles have to be surmounted.

1 For the classic definition of *rei interventus* and homologation see Bell's *Principles* paras 26 and 27; for a detailed discussion of *rei interventus* and homologation in relation to missives for the purchase and sale of heritable property see Cusine and Rennie *Missives* (1993) paras 2.06 ff.

There must be a preceding contract

3.04 The opening words of s 1(6) refer to a pre-existing contract, obligation or trust. Presumably this would be oral or partly oral and partly in writing. It is clear that it requires to be shown that some form of consensus has been reached and existing case law relating to *rei interventus* may well still be relevant here[1]. The agreement is capable of proof by any available evidence since the requirement for proof by writ or oath is abolished (s 11).

1 See *Mitchell v Stornoway Trustees* 1936 SC (HL) 56 at 63; *Stobo Ltd v Morrisons (Gowns) Ltd* 1949 SC 184; *East Kilbride Development Corporation v Pollok* 1953 SC 370; *Temperance Permanent Building Society v Kominek* 1951 SLT (Sh Ct) 58; *Cusine and Rennie* para 2.07.

The actings or omission must be in reliance on the agreement

3.05 The Act states that the new forms of personal bar apply where one of the parties has acted or refrained from acting 'in reliance on the contract, obligation or trust'. There must therefore be a clear connection between the actings or lack of actings and the contract. Earlier authority relating to *rei interventus* is of value as persuasive authority in this aspect of the new statutory provision[1]. In terms of Bell's definition, the actings had to be 'unequivocably referable to the agreement' but this is no longer part of the requirement[2].

1 *Mowat v Caledonian Banking Co* (1895) 23 R 270; *Danish Dairy Co v Gillespie* 1922 SC 656; *Pollok v Whiteford* 1936 SC 402; *Secretary of State for Scotland v Ravenstone Securities Ltd* 1976 SC 171; *Cusine and Rennie* para 2.08.
2 Report on Requirements of Writing (Scot Law Com No 112) para 2–42.

The actings must be known to and permitted by the other party

3.06 The Act states that the actings or omission to act must be 'with the knowledge and acquiescence of the other party'. The statutory wording again mirrors Bell's classic definition of *rei interventus*. It is of the essence of any doctrine of personal bar that the party seeking to withdraw knew of the actings of the other party or his or her omission to act. As Lord President Clyde put it[1] 'it is his permission or encouragement of such acting or abstention which is the kernel of the evidence of his presumed consent, in other words, the root of the personal bar pled against him'. The Act does not attempt to define 'knowledge and acquiescence' in any way. Actual knowledge and acquiescence may be difficult to prove and it is submitted that in some cases the court may have to accept that knowledge and acquiescence has to be presumed from the circumstances. This was certainly the case in relation to *rei interventus* but even presumed knowledge was difficult to establish[2]. Solicitors acting for parties should remember that their own knowledge may be attributed to their clients[3].

1 *Danish Dairy Co v Gillespie* 1922 SC 656 at 664.
2 See *Gardner v Lucas* (1877) 5 R 638.
3 *Danish Dairy Co v Gillespie*, above; *Heiton v Waverley Hydropathic Co* (1877) 4 R 830; *Cusine and Rennie* para 2.10.

There must be material consequences

3.07 Bell's definition of *rei interventus* required that the actings be 'not unimportant' and 'productive of alteration of circumstances, loss or inconvenience, though not irretrievable'. The new statutory provision also requires that the party seeking to uphold the contract, obligation or trust is and will be affected not only by his or her own action or inaction but also by the threatened withdrawal of the other party (s 1(4)). While this may be thought of as a rewording of Bell's definition it should be noted that whereas in Bell's definition the actings themselves required to be material or 'not unimportant', as well as the consequences in the new statutory provisions it is the consequences of the action or inaction and of the threatened withdrawal which must be material. There probably is a difference between 'not unimportant' and 'material', and the new provisions are therefore stricter here. One might argue of course that unimportant actings are unlikely to have material consequences but the use of the word 'material' suggests that the actings require to be more significant than under Bell's definition. Nevertheless, existing case law on what was sufficient loss or damage for the purposes of *rei interventus* may be persuasive authority in relation to the new statutory concept[1].

1 See *Keanie v Keanie* 1940 SC 549; *Rutterford Ltd v Allied Breweries* 1990 SLT 249; *Cusine and Rennie* para 2.11.

Homologation

3.08 The new statutory provisions do not appear to set out any statutory form of homologation, in that they refer only to actions or omissions to act on the part of the party seeking to enforce the contract, obligation or trust. The Scottish Law Commission could not see any role for homologation in the new scheme[1]. There is no mention of the legal effect of actings on the part of the party seeking to withdraw from the contract. It could be argued of course that the Act leaves the general law of personal bar intact[2] but some doubt may exist because of the wording used in s 1(5) where it is made clear that the new statutory provisions 'replace the rules of law known as *rei interventus and* homologation'. The authors' view is that the doctrine of personal bar still applies in circumstances where the party seeking to withdraw has by his or her actions led the other party to believe that the contract was being treated as valid and enforceable. For example, if the seller takes down the 'For sale' sign, vacates the property and hands in the keys to his solicitor along with the titles, all to the knowledge of the purchaser, that might well amount, under the old law, to homologation and therefore still count as personal bar.

1 See the Report on Requirements of Writing (Scot Law Com No 112) para 2.40.
2 For the classic definition of personal bar see *Gatty v Maclaine* 1921 SC (HL) 1.

Rei interventus *to conclude contracts*

3.09 The Act is silent in relation to that type of *rei interventus* which has in the past been held to conclude a contract where consensus is lacking. The application of this type of *rei interventus* was set out by Gloag in the following terms[1]:

'But the term *rei interventus* is also applied, though not so frequently to the case where parties have been in negotiation for a contract, and one of them has acted, and has been known and allowed to act, on the mistaken assumption that the negotiations had reached the point of a completed contract . . . But when *rei interventus* is relied upon in cases where parties have not arrived at any agreement, verbal or written, the rule that actings may bind them to a contract is not an exception to the general rule that contract requires agreement. The actings in question are evidence that agreement has been actually reached, although it has not been indicated in words or in other ways than by actings. In the former case (normal *rei interventus*) the actings render an agreement binding; in the latter they prove that an agreement was reached.'

It is not the function of this book to discusss whether Gloag's proposition is legally well founded or not. Suffice it to say that it was supported in the case *Errol v Walker*[2]. This case has been a subject of trenchant criticism[3]. The question is whether or not the new legislation, in sweeping away *rei interventus* for the purposes of requirements of writing, has also swept it away in relation to the constitution of an incomplete agreement. The report of the Scottish Law Commission on which the Act is based probably accepted that *Errol v Walker* represented the law[4]. While it may well have been the intention of the framers of the report and indeed the framers of the legislation to leave untouched this aspect of the law of *rei interventus*, the words of s 1(5) are fairly clear. The subsection states that the new statutory provisions 'replace the rules of law known as *rei interventus* and homologation'. The question is whether the new statutory provisions replace *rei interventus* for all purposes or only for the purposes with which the Act is concerned, namely the requirements of writing. It is the authors' view that the latter interpretation is probably correct. The new provisions relating to statutory personal bar only relate to a situation where there is a pre-existing agreement of sorts and apply where under the new provisions that agreement still requires to be in writing but had not been constituted in writing. We do not think that the new provisions will affect that type of *rei interventus* or personal bar which was described by Gloag and applied in *Errol v Walker*. The authors' view remains as it always has been, namely, that Gloag's proposition is not well founded in authority and that *Errol v Walker* is wrongly decided[5].

1 *The Law of Contract* (2nd edn, 1929, pp 46–47).
2 1966 SC 93.
3 AL Stewart (1966) 11 JLSS 263; SC Smith '*Rei interventus* Revisited' 1986 SLT (News) 137; Walker *Contract* para 13–36; McBryde *The Law of Contract in Scotland* (1987) para 27–44; *Cusine and Rennie* para 3.36.
4 Report on Requirements of Writing (Scot Law Com No 112) para 5–12.
5 See *Cusine and Rennie* paras 3.36 and 3.38.

Interest in land

3.10   The Act defines an 'interest in land' as 'any estate, interest or right in or over land including any right to occupy or to use land or to restrict the occupation or use of land' (s 1(7)). The term 'interest in land' does not, however, include a tenancy, a right to occupy or use land, or a right to restrict the occupation or use of land if such tenancy or right is not granted for more than one year, unless the tenancy or right is for a recurring period or periods and there is a gap of more than one year between the beginning of the first and end of the last of such periods (s 1(7)(a)–(c)). The term 'interest in land' does not include growing crops or moveable buildings or other moveable structures (s 1(8)(a) and (b)).

Subscription

3.11   Where a contract, obligation or trust requires to be in writing it must be subscribed (s 2(1)). The Act restates, with some additions and amendments, the existing law relating to subscription[1]. Except where some enactment provides other-wise, a document is subscribed by the granter if it is signed by him or her at the end of the last page of the deed excluding any inventory or annexation (s 7(1)). It should be noted that wills and other testamentary writings do not require to be signed on each page unless self-proving status is desired (s 3(2))[2].

1 See paras 2.05 ff.
2 See para 3.18.

Style of signature

3.12 An individual subscribes correctly in terms of the Act if he or she signs:
(1) his or her full name as set out in the document or testing clause; (s 7(2)(a)–(c)); or
(2) his or her surname preceded at least by one forename or ini-tial abbreviation or familiar form of a forename; or
(3) except where self-proving status is desired (s 3(2))[1], with another name which does not accord with the previous requirements or a description or an initial or a mark, pro-vided it can be established that the different name, description, initial or mark was that person's usual method of signing or his or her usual method of signing documents or alterations of the type in question or was intended by that person as his or her signature to the docu-ment or alteration.

This provision introduces the notion that a document can be subscribed by mark, initials or nickname. It should be noted, however, that this type of subscription will not suffice if it is intended that the deed should have self-proving status in terms of the Act.

1 See para 3.18.

Position of signature

3.13 In the normal way the signature is to be at the end of the last page of the document, but where there is more than one granter this requirement is complied with if at least one gran-ter signs the end of the last page and any other granter or gran-ters sign on an additional page (s 7(3)). The Act does not state that more than one additional page can be used.

Granter acting in different capacities

3.14 Where a person signs a document in more than one capacity it is sufficient for that person to sign only once and such a subscription binds that person in all capacities (s 7(4)).

Special persons

3.15 The Act preserves any existing rules in relation to the subscription or signing of documents by members of the royal family, by peers or by the wives or eldest sons of peers (ss 7(6), 13). It is well known that the Sovereign can superscribe and simply signs her Christian name with the letter R thereafter. Peers subscribe their title alone and if they have more than one title, they normally use their highest title, unless the deed in question has a particular connection with one of the subsidiary titles in which case it may be used in conjunction with the highest title. Wives of peers subscribe their husband's title prefixed by their own Christian names. Where the eldest son of a peer has a courtesy title he may subscribe by using that title. The method of execution of deeds by non-natural persons or special bodies is considered in Chapter 4.

Subscription must be voluntary

3.16 The Act makes no changes in the rules relating to the method of signature employed. The subscription must be the voluntary act of the granter[1].

1 See para 2.06.

Subscription by attorney

3.17 The Act preserves the right of a person to appoint an attorney with power to grant and subscribe deeds on behalf of that party (s 12(2)).

The new probativity

3.18 The Act does not use the word 'probative' at all. It does, however, retain the concept of probativity in the evidential sense of that term. Thus, even where writing is not required (far less attested writing), parties may choose to execute their documents in such a way as to render the fact of subscription by the granter self-proving. As with previous legislation going back to 1540 self-proving status is acquired by the use of a witness. The new Act provides that a document is presumed to have been subscribed by the granter if it has been subscribed by the granter, signed by a person as a witness, and the document or the testing clause or equivalent states the name and address of the witness, provided that nothing in the document or testing clause indicates that it was not so subscribed or was not validly witnessed (s 3(1)). Where a testamentary writing, such as a will, consists of more than one page, then it must be subscribed on each page to achieve self-proving status in addition to being witnessed (s 3(2)). The main change from previous law is that only one witness is required to achieve probativity. There are certain statutory formalities laid down in the Act in relation to witnessing.

The name and designation of the witness must be inserted

3.19   The name and address of a witness must appear in the deed, usually in the testing clause, but these can be added at any time before the document is founded on in legal proceedings or registered for preservation in the Books of Council and Session or in the sheriff court books. The name and designation of the witness need not be written by the witness himself (s 3(3)). Presumably the name and address should be added after the witness's signature.

The witness's signature must be genuine

3.20   Where it can be established in relation to a deed or document that the signature bearing to be that of a witness is not the signature of the witness, by reason of forgery or otherwise, then there is no presumption of probativity in respect of the subscription of the granter (s 3(4)(a)). This need not mean that the deed or document is invalid; it simply means that the subscription of the granter is not self-proving.

The witness must be competent

3.21 The Act provides that certain persons are not competent witnesses. These disqualifications are broadly similar to the disqualifications in force prior to the passing of the Act[1]. They are:

(1) A person who has already signed the document as a granter of it (s 3(4)(b)). Where a deed has been signed by several granters one of the granters cannot witness another granter's signature.

(2) A person who did not know the granter at the time of signing (s 3(4)(c)(i)). In the previous law, it was sufficient for the witness to be introduced to the granter at the time of subscription[2]. Presumably the same standard still applies. The Act itself states that the witness is regarded as having known the granter if he or she had credible information of the granter's identity at the time of witnessing (s 3(5)).

(3) A person under 16 (s 3(4)(c)(ii)).

(4) A person mentally incapable of acting as a witness (s 3(4)(c)(iii)).

It is interesting to note that the Act does not expressly exclude blind persons or persons who are unable to write. It is the view of the authors that both are excluded by implication. A blind person cannot witness a signature since he or she cannot see the granter sign nor connect any acknowledgment of subscription with a signature (s 3(4)(d)). A person who cannot write is not able to subscribe. A witness must comply with the same rules for the act of subscription as the granter, except that there is no relaxation of the rules which allows a witness to sign by mark or initials (s 7(5)).

1 See para 2.12.
2 *Brock v Brock* 1908 SC 964.

The act of witnessing

3.22 Under the Act a person witnesses the granter's subscription if he or she sees the granter subscribe or if the granter acknowledges his or her subscription to the witness (s 3(7)). If it can be established that the person who purports to be a witness did not in fact see the granter subscribe nor hear such an acknowledgment, then there is no presumption that the document has been subscribed and the subscription loses its self-proving status (s 3(4)(d)).

Time of witness's signature

3.23 The Act preserves the existing principle that self-proving status is achieved only by a single act of execution comprising the subscription of the granter and the subscription of the witness, with the whole process being carried out *unico contextu* (s 3(4)(e))[1]. The Act however does not suggest that the witness must act with the authority of the granter. This requirement was laid down in the decision of the House of Lords in *Walker v Whitwell*[2] where it was held that a person who had seen a granter sign could not sign as a witness after the death of the granter because all mandates fell on death. It still seems unlikely that a person who witnessed a deed by stealth without the knowledge of the granter could act as a witness and, although the Act does not preclude a witness from subscribing a deed after the death of the granter whose signature is being witnessed, it is unlikely that such an attempt at witnessing would satisfy the statutory requirement that the subscription of the granter and the subscription of the witness be one continuous process (s 3(4)(e)). Where a document is being granted by more than one granter, and one person is the witness to the subscription of more than one of the granters, then the subscription or acknowledgment of any granter and the witness's signature are not regarded as falling foul of the *unico contextu* rule, by reason only of the fact that all or some of the granters choose to sign the deed before the witness actually signs (s 3(6)).

1 See *Walker v Whitwell* 1916 SC (HL) 75; *Hynd's Trustee v Hynd's Trustees* 1955 SC (HL) 1.
2 1916 SC (HL) 75.

Inessential formalities – place and date of subscription

3.24 There is no requirement under the new law for the place or date of execution to be inserted in the deed. However, where a document or deed has the benefit of the new self-proving status under s 3(1) of the Act and the document or testing clause or equivalent bears to state the date or place of subscription, and there is nothing in the deed or testing clause to indicate that the statement as to date or place is incorrect, then there is a statutory presumption that the document was subscribed by the granter on the date and place stated (s 3(8)). This presumption also applies to wills and testamentary writings whether or not they have been witnessed under the Act (s 3(10)).

Defects in attestation

3.25 Under the previous law it was clear that a heavy burden of proof lay on any party who sought to reduce a deed because of some alleged defect in attestation especially where the signature of the granter was admitted[1]. It must now be borne in mind that probativity or self-proving status is no longer required for the constitution of contracts, deeds, obligations or trusts. Accordingly, even where there is a serious defect in attestation, as where a deed is witnessed by someone who is incompetent, the deed may remain valid. It is not probative or self-proving under the new rules but provided the subscription of the granter can be proved in some other way[2], this does not matter. It is thought that the onus on a party seeking to attack the attestation of a document is still heavy. The Act does refer to the possibility of establishing in proceedings that a person who signed a document as a witness did not in fact sign, whether by reason of forgery or otherwise (s 3(4)(a)); or that the person purporting to witness did not in fact witness the subscription (s 3(4)(d)); or that the execution was not carried out as one continuous process (s 3(4)(e)); or that the name or address of the witness was added after the document had been founded on or registered in the Books of Council and Session or sheriff court books (s 3(3)); or is erroneous in a material respect (s 3(4)(f)); or in the case of a testamentary document consisting of more than one sheet the signature on any sheet bearing to be the testator's signature is not the testator's signature whether by reason of forgery or otherwise (s 3(4)(g)). However, given the fact that the Act preserves the

notion of probativity in the sense of a self-proving subscription, it is unlikely that the attestation of a deed which appears
to have been properly witnessed will be easily attacked.

1 Halliday *Conveyancing Law and Practice in Scotland* (1985) vol I, para 3–16; *Smith v
  Bank of Scotland* (1824) 2 Sh App 265, HL at 286 and 287; *Sibbald v Sibbald* (1776)
  Mor 16906; *Forrest v Low's Trustees* 1907 SC 1240.
2 See para 3.28.

Style of witness's signature

3.26 A document is properly signed by a witness if it is
signed using:
(1) the full name of the witness as shown in the document or
    testing clause; or
(2) the witness's surname, preceded by at least one forename
    or an initial or abbreviation or familiar form of a forename
    (s 7(5)).
Where the witness is witnessing the signature of more than one
granter, the witness need sign only once (s 7(5)). It should be
noted that there is no provision in the Act for a witness to sign by
mark, initial or by an unusual name or nickname. The relaxation
provided in relation to the subscription of deeds by granters
does not appear to apply to subscription of deeds by witnesses.

Annexations, plans and inventories

3.27 Prior to the passing of the 1995 Act, all inventories, annexations and plans were required to be subscribed by the granter of
the deed on the last page of any such annexation or inventory.
Plans required to be subscribed. Where formal documents were
being executed with more than one schedule this sometimes
caused difficulty and the practice arose of having only one
schedule split into various parts, so that only one set of signatures was required at the end of the schedule. The 1995 Act provides, with certain exceptions, that an annexation to a document
is incorporated in the document if it is referred to in the document and identified on its face as being the annexation referred
to, whether or not it is signed or subscribed (s 8(1)).
   This relaxation, however, does not apply where the document relates to land and the annexation describes or shows all
or any part of the land to which the document relates. In this

case, the annexation is regarded as incorporated only if it is referred to in the document, is identified on the face of the annexation as being the annexation referred to, and is signed on each page where it is a plan, drawing, photograph or representation, or on the last page where it is an inventory, appendix, schedule or other writing (s 8(2)). Where the annexation is to a document relating to land and therefore requires to be signed, it is presumed to have been signed by the person who subscribes the document as granter (s 8(3)). The statutory requirements in relation to the style of signature apply equally to a signature to an annexation or plan (s 8(4)). Where an annexation does require to be signed, it can be signed at any time before the document is founded on in legal proceedings, registered for preservation in the Books of Council and Session or sheriff court books, recorded in the Register of Sasines or registered in the Land Register (s 8(5)). In land registration cases, the Keeper does accept plans which are signed after the date of acknowledgment of the original application for registration, as where an incorrect plan given in with a deed is replaced. It is the authors' view that the statutory provisions still allow for this practice, given the fact that the registration process is not completed until the Keeper is satisfied, although the date of registration is the date of original acknowledgment. Where there is more than one granter of a deed and the annexation requires to be signed on the last page, it is regarded as having been signed on the last page provided at least one granter signs at the end of the last page. Other granters may sign on an additional page of the annexation (s 8(6)).

Applications to the court for self-proving status

3.28 Under the previous law, a document was either probative or it was not probative. If it was improbative, *rei interventus* or homologation might be used in circumstances where probative writing was necessary for the constitution of the document. Section 4 of the 1995 Act introduces a new concept of certification of self-proving status by the court. Where a document bears to have been subscribed by a granter but has not been witnessed, so that it does not have self-proving status under s 3 of the Act, the court may, on the application of any person having an interest in the document, cause the document to be endorsed with a certificate to the effect that it has been subscribed by the granter (s 4(1)(a)). Where the document has already been registered in the Books of Council and Session or sheriff court Books, the court may grant a decree to that effect (s 4(1)(b)). Similarly, where a document bears to have been subscribed by the granter but there is no presumption as to the date or place of subscription, the court may, on an application being made by any person having an interest in the document, cause the document to be endorsed with a certificate that the place and date of subscription indicated in the deed are accurate (s 4(2)(a)); or again where the document has been registered in the Books of Council and Session or sheriff court Books grant a decree to that effect (s 4(2)(b)). In all cases, the evidence is by way of affidavit unless the court otherwise directs (s 4(3)). Applications to the court for certification or decree either as to subscription by the granter or as to the place and date of subscription are by summary application, or as an incidental motion in the course of other proceedings (s 4(4)).

The effect of a certificate or decree is to create a presumption that the document has been subscribed by the granter concerned or a presumption that the statement in the certificate or decree as to the date or place of subscription is accurate (s 4(5)). The 'court', under this section, in the case of a summary application means the sheriff in whose sheriffdom the applicant resides, or where the applicant does not reside in Scotland, the sheriff at Edinburgh (s 4(5)(a)). If, however, the application is made as an incidental application in the course of other proceedings, then the court dealing with these proceedings can deal with the matter and grant the necessary certificate or decree as to subscription or place and date of subscription if it considers it appropriate to do so (s 4(6)(b)). This new provision may well prove useful in cases where a document is being founded on or produced in court, but does not have self-proving status due to a lack of a witness or some defect in the witnessing.

The Act does not give any guidance as to what type of evidence is required in these cases. The court has to be satisfied that the document was subscribed, or, if the application relates to the place and date of subscription, that the document was indeed subscribed at the place and on the date specified. Clearly, if a party actually witnessed the signature of the granter but did not sign as a witness, that party could grant an affidavit. Apart from this, parties who know the granter's handwriting might also grant affidavits to the effect that the signature is that of the granter. It appears that affidavits from two persons are required. Certainly, in the context of holograph wills confirmation is not granted unless there are affidavits from two persons regarding the handwriting. That is provided for in the Succession (Scotland) Act 1964, s 24 which is not amended by the 1995 Act. We therefore assume that two affidavits are required for each granter's signature. Affidavits in relation to the place and time of subscription may be more problematic, unless they are granted by persons who actually saw the granter subscribe or who can fix the place and date of subscription in some other way.

Documents requiring registration

3.29 Although the Act abolishes any requirement that a document must be witnessed to be valid, there is one case where even under the new provisions attestation by one witness is required. In terms of s 6 of the Act, it is not competent to record a document in the Register of Sasines nor register it for execution or preservation in the Books of Council and Session or sheriff court books unless the subscription of the document has self-proving status under s 3, by virtue of attestation by one witness, or has been certified by the court in terms of s 4 (s 6(1)). Where a document has been granted by more than one granter, it is competent to record or register that document if the subscription of at least one granter is self-proving, either by attestation or certification (s 6(2)). Certain types of document which must be recorded in the Register of Sasines or Books of Council and Session or sheriff court books are exempt from the requirement of attestation or certification. These are (s 6(3)):

(1) Documents where recording or registration is required or expressly permitted under any enactment (s 6(3)(a)).
(2) Decrees which are to be recorded in the Register of Sasines (s 6(3)(b)), for example a decree of reduction.

(3) Testamentary documents registered in the Books of Council and Session or sheriff court books (s 6(3)(c)(i)).

(4) Documents directed by the Court of Session or sheriff court to be registered in the Books of Council and Session or sheriff court books (s 6(3)(c)(ii).

(5) Documents whose formal validity is governed by a law other than Scots law which are to be registered in the Books of Council and Session or sheriff court books if the Keeper of the Registers or sheriff clerk is satisfied that the document is formally valid according to the law governing its validity (s 6(3)(c)(iii)).

(6) A court decree to be registered in the Books of Council and Session or sheriff court books, for certification as to the granter's subscription or the place and date of signature of the deed or in relation to any alteration to the deed, in terms of ss 4 or 5 of the Act where this relates to a document which has already been registered in the Books of Council and Session or in the sheriff court books (s 6(3)(c)(iv)).

(7) The registration of any court decree in a separate register maintained expressly for that purpose (s 6(3)(d)), for example, foreign judgments.

The Act formally reiterates the principle that a document may be registered for preservation in the Books of Council and Session or the sheriff court books without a clause of consent to registration (s 6(4)).

Registration in the Land Register

3.30   The Act does not mention registration of deeds or documents in the Land Register nor does it require that such deeds be self-proving in terms of ss 3 or 4 of the Act. The Keeper already has a statutory discretion as to what documents he is prepared to accept as evidence of title in the Land Register[1]. It is likely, however, that documents where the subscription has self-proving status in so far as matters of title are concerned will be insisted on, otherwise the Keeper might have to form a judgment about the genuineness or accuracy of the subscription. There is no reason why the Keeper should wish to put his indemnity at risk and the practice of having deeds relating to heritable property subscribed and attested by a witness is certain to continue whether or not the property lies in an operational area for land registration purposes.

1 Land Registration (Scotland) Act 1979, s 4(1).

Summary of the modern requirements

3.31   Professor Halliday gave a convenient summary of the requirements for execution of probative deeds by natural persons as at 31 December 1984[1] which has applied until the passing of the new Act. It is convenient to summarise the requirements for self-proving status under the new Act.

(1) The deed must be subscribed by the granter or granters and any consenting party on the last page of an ordinary deed. A testamentary writing such as a will must be subscribed on every page where it consists of a deed of more than one sheet.

(2) The granter must subscribe his or her own name in full or by surname preceded by initials or contractions representing the forenames. Initials or a mark or a nickname does not suffice if the subscription is to be self-proving.

(3) If there is an annexation to the document then it is incorporated in the document if it is referred to in the document and identified in the document as being the annexation referred to, whether or not it is signed, unless the document relates to land and the annexation describes or shows all or any part of the land, in which case the annexation also requires to be signed on each page if it is a plan, drawing, photograph or representation, or on the last page where it is an inventory or other type of appendix or schedule.

(4) Where there is more than one granter it is sufficient if at least one granter signs at the end of the last page of the document or last page of any appendix, and other granters may sign on an additional signing page.

(5) The granter and any consenter must sign in the presence of, or acknowledge his or her signature to, one competent witness who subscribes his or her normal signature on the last page of the deed as attestation.

(6) The witness must be named and designed by address in the deed, normally in a testing clause or equivalent docquet or, alternatively, the name and address can still be

added after the witness's signature by the witness or
another party prior to the deed being founded on or registered in the Books of Council and Session or sheriff court
books.

(7) As an alternative to attestation by one witness, the subscription can achieve self-proving status if a court grants a
certificate or decree to the effect that it has been subscribed
by the granter.

1 *Halliday* vol 1, para 3–04.

Notarial execution

3.32 The Requirements of Writing (Scotland) Act 1995
repeals in its entirety s 18 of the Conveyancing (Scotland) Act
1924 relating to notarial execution. Section 9 of the new Act
coupled with Schedule 3 set out the new provisions relating to
execution of deeds on behalf of parties who are blind or unable
to write. The section provides that where the granter declares
that he or she is blind or unable to write, then a person having
authority to do so in terms of the section (a 'relevant person')
may subscribe on behalf of that granter. It should be noted
that as before a blind person is still entitled to sign a deed
himself or herself (s 9(7))[1]. The new provisions do not refer to
notaries as such but to a 'relevant person'. It is the relevant
person who can subscribe on behalf of the granter. Normally
the document is read over verbatim by the relevant person
to the granter. The Act, however, does allow the granter to
make a declaration that he or she does not require the document read over to him or her, in which case the deed can be
subscribed by the relevant person without reading it to the
granter at all (s 9(1)(b)). In such a case we suggest that the
notary or other relevant person takes some steps to acquaint
the granter with the main provisions of the deed. In the case of
testamentary documents, it might be prudent to read the
whole document. The declaration by the granter waiving the
requirement that the deed be read verbatim must be noted in
the testing clause, because there is no provision for any docquet of any sort to be added to the deed by the relevant person. The relevant person simply subscribes the deed using his

or her signature in the normal way. The new provisions make no express provision for witnessing because self-proving subscription of documents is required only in certain restricted cases (s 6)[2]. Accordingly, the only requirement is that the subscription by the relevant person should take place in the presence of the granter (s 9(2)). Schedule 3 to the Act applies the provisions of the Act relating to self-proving status to documents which have been subscribed by a relevant person with the authority of the granter. Basically what this means is that the relevant person's execution can be made self-proving if it is witnessed in the normal way by a competent witness. In the case of a will or testamentary writing the relevant person requires to sign each page. There is an additional requirement in the case of notarial execution that the witness must also see the granting of authority by the granter to the relevant person and the reading of the document to the granter by the relevant person, or the declaration by the granter that this is not required (Sch 3, para 4(dd)). The Schedule also applies with appropriate modifications s 4(1) of the Act, so that a court can accord an execution by a relevant person self-proving status by certificate or decree. Schedule 3 also applies with appropriate amendments the various parts of the Act which deal with alterations and interlineations to notarially executed documents.

1 See *Duff v Earl of Fife* (1823) 1 Shaw's App 498.
2 See para 3.29.

Who may execute deeds notarially?

3.33 The deed or document may be executed on behalf of the granter by a solicitor holding a practising certificate, an advocate, a justice of the peace or a sheriff clerk, and in relation to the execution of documents outwith Scotland, by a notary public or any other person with official authority under the law of the place of execution to execute documents on behalf of persons who are blind or unable to write (s 9(6)). There was some debate as to whether the category of persons entitled to carry out notarial executions should be extended or restricted. At one time there was a view that only solicitors should be allowed to subscribe deeds on behalf of others. Parish ministers have now been removed from the category of persons entitled to execute deeds on behalf of other parties and no distinction is now made between ordinary documents and testamentary documents.

Who may use notarial execution?

3.34 The Act makes no change in the categories of persons who may use notarial execution in that it again specifies those who are blind or unable to write (s 9(1))[1] and the Act omits the previous wording of the Conveyancing (Scotland) Act 1924, s 18 which referred to any person who was blind or unable to write from any cause whether temporary or permanent. The omission of these words does not restrict the categories of people who may use notarial execution. The requirement is that the person makes a declaration that he or she is blind or unable to write. The cause and the duration of the disability are therefore not relevant.

1 See para 3.32.

Procedure

3.35 Procedure varies depending on whether it is desired to execute a deed where the execution is self-proving or not. In any event the previous rule, that the whole procedure should be carried through as one continuous process, remains. Even where a witness is not involved, the subscription by the relevant person must take place in the presence of the granter (s 9(2)). Where it is desired to have a self-proving execution and a witness is therefore involved, the granter, the relevant person and the witness must be together and the witness must hear the appropriate authority given and see the relevant person sign (Sch 3, para 2[1]). The witness must also hear the deed read over to the granter or alternatively hear the granter give appropriate authority to dispense with this formality (Sch 3, para 2[1]). Clearly the witness should sign immediately after the relevant person has signed. Annexations to documents may also be signed by the relevant person subject to the modifications set out in Schedule 3 (s 9(5)). Accordingly, where the document is read over to the granter then any plan, drawing, photograph and other representation contained in an annexation should be described by the relevant person to the granter (s 9(5)). Although there is no docquet, the document or testing clause or equivalent must state that the document was read over to the granter by the relevant person or that the granter dispensed with that formality (Sch 3, para 2[2]).

1 Applying s 3(1).
2 Applying s 3(1)(b).

Disqualifying interest

3.36 The new provisions do not abolish the previous rule that the person carrying out the execution on behalf of the granter should be independent and disinterested. It has long been recognised, however, that the strict rule relating to disqualifying interest which invalidated the whole deed merely punished the parties to the deed, be they the granter who frequently was by then deceased or the beneficiary[1]. Parties relying on notarial execution cannot really be expected to know the strict rules which apply and it is unfair that a deed signed on their behalf should be denied effect because of the ignorance or malpractice of the notary or relevant person. Accordingly, the new provisions merely provide that where the document confers on the 'relevant person or his [or her] spouse, son or daughter a benefit in money or money's worth (whether directly or indirectly)', it 'shall be invalid to the extent, but only to the extent, that it confers such benefit' (s 9(4)). It is interesting to note that the category of benefited persons is restricted to close relatives. A benefit to a live-in partner of the relevant person is presumably not struck at.

The effect of this provision is that if the remainder of the deed can be separated it receives effect and only the benefit to the relevant person is invalidated. If, for example, the relevant person was the grantee, or sole beneficiary, the whole deed would fall. The Act does not give any guidance as to the meaning of a benefit in money or money's worth. Presumably a purely fiduciary appointment as trustee with no power to charge fees is not struck at. It is clearly still preferable to use an independent notary or relevant person, and essential if the notary or relevant person has an entitlement to charge fees or share in fees as part of the testamentary settlement. The existing case law is still relevant in deciding what may or may not be a direct or indirect benefit, but only the benefit is invalidated under the new legislation[2]. A benefit to a partner of the relevant person where that benefit is shared as partnership profit is still struck at.

The new provisions do not refer to the situation where more than one party to the deed is blind or unable to write. While it is unlikely, given the new provisions in relation to disqualifying interest, that a deed would be invalidated if one notary or relevant person subscribed on behalf of both parties, it is probably still undesirable that this should happen and independent notaries or relevant persons should act for each[3].

1 See *Halliday* vol I, para 3–39, footnote 20.
2 See para 2.31; *Ferrie v Ferrie's Trustees* (1863) 1 M 291; *Newstead v Dansken* 1918 1 SLT 136; *Finlay v Finlay's Trustees* 1948 SC 16; *Gorrie's Trustees v Stiven's Executrix* 1952 SC 1; *Crawford's Trustees v Glasgow Royal Infirmary* 1955 SC 367.
3 See *Craig v Richardson* (1610) Mor 16829; *Graeme v Graeme's Trustees* (1868) 7 M 14; *Lang v Lang's Trustees* (1889) 16 R 590.

Forms of testing clause

3.37 The Act makes specific provision for the retention of a testing clause as a means of providing information relating to the execution of a document, including the name and address of the witness, place and date of signing and details of any notarial execution (s 10(1)). The Act also provides that the Secretary of State may prescribe by regulation the form of such a testing clause from time to time (s 10(1)). Different forms of testing clause may be prescribed for different cases or classes of case (s 10(2)). This does not mean that a testing clause is obligatory in every case where a document has been witnessed or where it is desired to provide some information such as place or date of signature or details of a notarial execution. The provision is without prejudice to the effectiveness of any other means of providing information relating to the execution of a document. In its Report the Scottish Law Commission has 'Model Forms of Testing Clause' (Appendix B) which differ from those currently in use. A testing clause is not invalid even if it does not conform to the Secretary of State's prescribed form, provided all the requisite information is contained therein. It is clearly still competent to add the address of the witness after the signature of the witness (ss 10(1) and 3(3)).

Abolition of proof by writ or oath, *obligationes literis* and privileged writings

3.38 Given the fact that one of the main provisions of the Act is to abolish the necessity of writing for the formation of contracts except in certain cases, any rule of law and any enactment whereby the proof of any matter is restricted to proof by writ or oath is abolished, as is the procedure of proving any matter in civil proceedings by reference to an oath (s 11(1), (2)). Similarly, the requirement that certain contracts be formed in writing is abolished without prejudice, of course, to the requirements of the Act itself in this regard (s 11(3)(a)). The status of privileged writings such as holograph documents, documents which have been adopted as holograph and documents *in re mercatoria* is abolished. Clearly the framers of the Act take the view that there is no need to have any special status for these documents within the new provisions. The abolition of holograph status has caused some disquiet, particularly among members of the legal profession where there has been a long-established practice of concluding missives in relation to heritable property by way of letters which are adopted as holograph. Under the new provisions missives can simply be constituted in writing. There is no requirement that they be constituted in attested writing given the fact that they are not normally registered or recorded. The concern which has been expressed is that there will be nothing to separate the missives from other informal correspondence on the file. Clearly some steps will require to be taken in this regard on a practical level. The likelihood is that legal practitioners will require missives to be constituted as a self-proving contract. If this is the case they will require attestation by one witness[1].

1 For a fuller discussion of the implications of the abolition of holograph status see *Cusine and Rennie* paras 2.20 ff.

Alterations in documents

3.39 As noted in Chapter 2 different considerations applied to alterations in deeds depending on whether the changes took place prior to or after execution. Similarly, in the case of testamentary deeds, there were a different set of rules depending on whether or not the alterations could be said to have been made *animo revocandi*[1]. The new Act applies to alterations made both before and after subscription and in relation to alterations made prior to subscription provides first that such alterations shall form part of the documents so subscribed (s 5(1)(a)), and secondly that such alterations may be proved by any competent evidence whether written or oral (s 5(3)). So far as alterations made after subscription are concerned, the Act states that these shall form part of the document if the alteration is signed by the granter or granters and the document in its altered form is formally valid (s 5(1)(b)). In the case of a self-proving document, any alteration may be presumed to have been made prior to subscription if the testing clause or the document states that the alteration was made before subscription and nothing in the document or testing clause indicates the contrary (s 5(5)). Alternatively, where the deed is not self-proving or the testing clause does not contain a suitable declaration, an application may be made to the court to have it certify that the alteration was made prior to subscription (s 5(6)). In any such application to the court the provisions of s 4 of the Act apply (s 5(7)).

1 See paras 2.20ff.

3.40 When an alteration is made to a document after it has been subscribed, Schedule 1 to the Act applies in relation to certain presumptions as to the self-proving nature of the alteration and the document in its altered form. Basically, what the Schedule provides is that if the alteration bears to have been signed by the granter and one competent witness, then it shall be presumed that the alteration was signed by that granter. Similar presumptions apply in the case of the place and the date of signature of the alteration. As with the execution of testamentary deeds, where the alteration is to a testamentary deed and consists of more than one sheet, the signature on the alteration will not be presumed unless each sheet of the alteration is signed (Sch 1, para 1(2)). As with self-proving status in relation to the execution of deeds themselves, the Schedule provides that if the alteration is not witnessed, application can be made to the court for a certificate that the alteration was in fact subscribed (Sch 1, para 2). For the purposes of the Schedule, the rules in relation to the competence of witnesses and the act of witnessing itself are the same as for the execution and attestation of deeds.

Special provisions and testamentary writings

3.41 The provisions of the Act and the Schedules do not affect the law on erasures contained in the Erasures in Deeds (Scotland) Act 1836 or the little, if ever, used s 54 of the Conveyancing (Scotland) Act 1874 (s 5(2)(b)). Nor does the Act affect any rule which allows a testamentary provision to be revoked by deletion or erasure without that deletion or erasure being authenticated (s 5(2)(a))[1].

1 See para 2.25 and *Pattison's Trustees v the University of Edinburgh* (1886) 16 R 73.

Practical considerations

3.42 The authors cannot help but feel that the new provisions in relation to the authentication of alterations made after subscription may prove somewhat cumbersome. It is not easy to sidescribe alterations, far less have them witnessed. However, the provisions of the Act in relation to alterations which have been made prior to subscription are relatively simple to operate. It appears that if the deed itself has self-proving status already and there is an alteration or addition, then all that needs happen is that the alteration or addition be noted in the testing clause, provided nothing in the document or testing clause indicates that the alteration was made after subscription (s 5(5)). Practitioners are of course readily aware of the legal fictions perpetrated in many testing clauses. While the authors may be accused of a certain degree of cynicism, it is their view that most alterations will certainly appear to have taken place prior to subscription.

CHAPTER 4

The law after 1995 – execution of deeds by persons other than natural persons

Introduction

4.01 Chapter 2 dealt with the execution of deeds by partnerships[1], local authorities[2], building societies[3], companies[4] and other statutory bodies[5], and probativity. The 1995 Act deals with these issues in relation to partnerships, companies, local authorities, other bodies corporate, and Ministers of the Crown and office-holders.

Four things should be borne in mind. First, in each case (with the exception of companies) the pattern of the Act is to require only one signature where a signature is required and, if the document is to be self-proving, that the signature should be witnessed by one witness or the seal, where the body has one, should be affixed. Secondly, the Act sets out the basic minimum requirements, and therefore it is open to any body to insist on more than the minimum requirements for its internal purposes, but if a deed complies with the provisions of the Act that will suffice. Thirdly, the Act does not deal with other unincorporated bodies, such as clubs, and it is still necessary for these bodies to address the question of how deeds are to be executed on their behalf. Lastly, if any statute which is not amended by the 1995 Act makes special provision for the execution of deeds by any of the bodies dealt with by the 1995 Act, that provision, and not the 1995 Act, has to be complied with. That is made clear by the opening words of the various parts of Schedule 2[6]. Each of the bodies mentioned are now dealt with.

1 Para 2.07.
2 Para 2.08.
3 Para 2.09.
4 Para 2.10.
5 Para 2.11.
6 Paras 2(1), (2); 3(1); 4(1); 5(2) and 6(1).

Partnerships

4.02 Until 1995 a distinction had to be drawn between deeds executed by a partner, where the transactions were in the ordinary course of the business of the firm, and other transactions; and in relation to the latter, all the partners had to sign. The 1995 Act does not alter either s 5 of the Partnership Act 1890 (power to a partner to bind a firm) nor s 6 (partners bound by acts on behalf of a firm). Accordingly, it is still essential to consider the question of authority. However, the 1995 Act simplifies matters by providing that a document (or an alteration to the document) is validly executed on behalf of a partnership if it is signed by one partner or another authorised person[1]. The person signing may use either his or her own name, or the firm name[2].

If the partner is executing a document in a transaction which is in the ordinary course of the business of the firm, eg a partner in a solicitors' firm signing missives, authority is presumed by virtue of the 1890 Act, s 5. His or her signature is therefore a valid signature on behalf of the firm, and no further inquiry is necessary. If, however, a partner is signing a document in a transaction which is not in the ordinary course of the business of the firm, for example a sale of the firm's heritable property, or someone other than a partner is signing any document in connection with any transaction on behalf of the firm, it is necessary to establish that the partner or other person has the requisite authority under s 5 or s 6 of the 1890 Act, but having ascertained that the authority exists, the signature of that individual is a valid execution on behalf of the firm. The doubt which arose in *Littlejohn v MacKay*[3] about whether missives could be signed on behalf of a firm by the manager of the firm who was not a partner, but who had general authority to act on behalf of the firm, has now been removed.

It should be borne in mind that the 1995 Act does not deal with the title to heritable property belonging to a partnership which devolves in accordance with the law of trusts[4]. The title to heritage which is partnership property stands in the name of trustees and so all the trustees, or a quorum, must execute any deed.

1 Sch 2, para 2(1)(3).
2 Sch 2, para 3.
3 1974 SLT (Sh Ct) 82.
4 Partnership Act 1890, s 2.

Companies

4.03 The pattern established for individuals has been replicated for companies also[1] but the Act recognises the commercial need to have provisions regarding the execution of deeds by companies which are the same north and south of the border, a point to which we shall return. Following the pattern of the earlier provisions, the Act provides that a deed[2], or an alteration to a deed[3] or a post-execution alteration to a deed[4] is validly executed by a company if it is signed by one director, or the secretary, or by a person authorised to sign the document on its behalf. If there is no secretary, or the secretary is unable to act, the assistant or deputy secretary may act, or if neither of these exists or is unable to act, any officer who has general authority or specific authority may act[5]. The 1995 Act specifically states that this provision does not affect the powers of receivers, administrators, administrative receivers, or liquidators[6] and as pointed out below[7], the powers of judicial factors are not affected either. So far as self-proving status is concerned the Act provides, as in the case of individuals, that the signature of the director etc may be witnessed by a single witness[8] and the name and address of the witness may be stated in the deed or the testing clause or its equivalent[8]. However, the deed will also be self-proving if it is signed by two directors, or a director and the secretary, or by two authorised persons[8].

1 Sch 2, para 3.
2 Sch 2, para 3(1).
3 Sch 2, para 3(3).
4 Sch 1, para 1, substituted by Sch 2, para 3(6).
5 Companies Act 1985, s 283(3).
6 Sch 2, para 3(2) making reference to the Insolvency Act 1986, Sch 1, para 9; Sch 2, para 9 and Sch 4, para 7.
7 See para 4.05.
8 S 3(1), substituted by Sch 2, para 3(5)(a).

4.04 As mentioned above, the Act recognises that it is commercially expedient for the requirements for execution etc of deeds in Scotland to be the same as in England and Wales. That view was recognised in the provisions of the Companies Act 1985, s 36B. In order to achieve this the 1995 Act provides that if the signature is not witnessed the deed is deemed to have been executed by the company (ie it is self-proving) if it is subscribed on behalf of the company by two directors, a director and the secretary, or two persons authorised to subscribe the document on its behalf. In dealing with authorised persons, the Act uses the phrase 'authorised to sign the document or authorised to subscribe the document'[1]. At first sight that might suggest that these persons require authorisation in relation to each document, but the Act defines 'authorised' as meaning 'expressly or impliedly authorised and any reference to a person authorised to sign includes a reference to a person authorised to sign generally or in relation to a particular document'[3]. That said, the Act does provide that there is no presumption that a person purporting to sign as a director or the secretary is the holder of either office, and there is equally no presumption that the person subscribing as an authorised person is so authorised.

Thus, anyone dealing with a company is entitled to proof that a person purporting to be a director, secretary etc is the holder of the particular office, and proof that the person who purports to be authorised is so authorised. This is not a change in the law from the Companies Act 1985. Although an authorised person may be given specific or general authority to sign deeds on behalf of the company, anyone dealing with such a person is entitled to proof of that authority. However, once it is established that the person is authorised it is not necessary to ascertain whether he or she has specific authority in relation to the particular transaction, because that is presumed by virtue of the definition of 'authorised'. If the deed does not bear to have been witnessed, but bears to have been signed by two directors, or a director and the secretary, or two authorised persons, while it would normally have the benefit of being self-proving, that is not the case if it is proved that it has not been so signed, because the signatures, or one of them, are forgeries, or for some other reason the signatures are invalid[3]. Similar provisions are made for subscribing post-execution alterations, and in relation to self-proving status. Thus, such an alteration may be signed by a director, or the secretary, or by some other authorised person[4]. In order to be self-proving the signature must be witnessed (and the name of the witness may be in the document or in the testing clause or its equivalent)[5] but the alteration is also self-proving if it is signed on behalf of the company by two directors, or one director and the secretary, or two persons authorised to sign the alteration[6]. However, this presumption does not include a presumption that the person signing the alteration was a director, the secretary, or authorised[7] and accordingly one is still entitled to evidence to that effect.

The 1995 Act deals only with the execution of deeds by a director, the secretary or other authorised individuals and because of the definition of 'authorised'[8] and the references to the Insolvency Act 1986, the 1995 Act also governs execution of deeds by administrators, administrative receivers, receivers and liquidators[9].

1 Sch 2, para 3(1) and (5).
2 s 12(1).
3 s 3(4)(h), substituted by Sch 2, para 3(5).
4 Sch 1, para 1(1), substituted by Sch 2, para 3(6).
5 Sch 1, para 1(1)(a), (b), substituted by Sch 2, para 3(6).
6 Sch 1, para 1(1), (1A), substituted by Sch 2, para 3(6).
7 Sch 1, para 1(1), (1C), substituted by Sch 2, para 3(6).
8 s 12.
9 Sch 2, para 3(2), referring to the Insolvency Act 1986, Sch 1, para 9; Sch 2, para 9 and Sch 4.

4.05   The Act does not deal specifically with judicial factors, who can still competently be appointed at common law as an alternative to appointing a provisional liquidator, for example where there is a fear that the assets of the company might disappear[1]. However, it is submitted that by the appointment such a judicial factor becomes a person 'authorised' in terms of s 12 and hence someone who can execute deeds on behalf of the company and must comply with the terms of the 1995 Act, but, by so complying, has the benefit of the presumption of self-proving status to which the Act gives rise.

1 *McGuinness v Black (No 2)* 1990 SLT 461; *Palmer on Company Law* (1991) para 8–910.

Local authorities[1]

4.06   A document, or an alteration to a document, is validly executed on behalf of a local authority if it is signed by the proper officer[2], and a person who purports to sign as the proper officer is presumed to be the proper officer[3]. One hopes that despite this presumption local authorities will not be reluctant to provide proof that a person is the proper officer. In order to be self-proving, the document requires to appear to have been subscribed by the proper officer on behalf of the authority and to have either the signature of a witness to the proper officer's signature, or be sealed with the local authority seal[4]. The name and address of the witness may be in the document, or in any testing clause or the equivalent[5]. If the document does not appear to have been subscribed on behalf of the authority, or not validly witnessed[6] or where there is a seal and it can be shown that the seal was put on without authority, or was affixed on a date different from that of the subscription by the proper officer, then the document is not presumed to have been validly executed[7]. Similar provisions apply to post-execution alterations to the document. If the alteration appears to have been signed by the proper officer on behalf of the authority and it is witnessed or sealed, and there is nothing in the deed or the testing clause or its equivalent which indicates otherwise, the alteration is presumed to have been signed by the proper officer and by the authority[8]. If it can be shown that the alteration was not signed by the proper officer on behalf of the authority, or the alteration was not validly witnessed[9] or where there is no witness, but there is a seal, and it can be shown either that the seal was put on the deed without authority, or it was affixed on a date other than the date of subscription by the proper officer[10] then the presumption does not arise.

1 The definition is in the Local Government (Scotland) Act 1973, s 235(1) and is a council under the Local Government (Scotland) Act 1994, s 2.
2 Sch 2, para 4(1) and (3). This is normally the chief executive.
3 Sch 3, para 4(2).
4 s 3(1)(b), substituted by Sch 2, para 4(5).
5 s 3(1A), substituted by Sch 2, para 4(5).
6 s 3(1)(c), substituted by Sch 2, para 4(5).
7 s 3(4)(g), substituted by Sch 2, para 4(6).
8 Sch 1, para 1(1)(a), (b), substituted by Sch 2, para 4(7).
9 Sch 1, para 1(1)(c), substituted by Sch 2, para 4(7).
10 Sch 1, para 1(4)(h), substituted by Sch 2, para 4(8).

Other bodies corporate

4.07   In relation to other bodies corporate, similar provisions apply to execution[1], alterations[2], post-execution alterations[3], and self-proving status⁴. The person who signs on behalf of such a body is either a member of the governing board, or a member of the body⁵ or the secretary⁶ or a person authorised to sign on its behalf⁷. Unlike local authorities there is no presumption that the person signing is the person he or she purports to be, and so in each case⁸ it is necessary to ascertain that the person is a member of the board, member, or secretary, as the case may be, or otherwise authorised to sign on behalf of the body. These provisions apply to friendly societies, trade unions, the Bank of Scotland, and universities.

1 Sch 2, para 5(2), (4)–(6).
2 Sch 2, para 5(3).
3 Sch 2, para 5(7).
4 Sch 2, para 5(5), (7), (8).
5 Sch 2, para 5(2)(a).
6 Sch 2, para 5(2)(b).
7 Sch 2, para 5(2)(c).
8 s 3(1B), substituted by Sch 2, para 5(4).

Ministers of the Crown, etc

4.08 Once again, the Act contains similar provisions in relation to the execution of deeds etc by a Minister of the Crown and office-holders¹. What has been said above in relation to local authorities applies here², subject to the following points. A document is validly executed by a Minister or office-holder if it is signed personally³. It is also validly executed if there is by statute or other rule of law an officer or other Minister who may sign on behalf of the Minister and that officer signs⁴ or if a statute or other rule of law enacts that an officer of an office-holder may sign on behalf of the office-holder, and that officer signs⁵ or it is signed by some other person authorised to sign on behalf of the Minister or office-holder⁶. A person who purports to sign a deed, or an alteration, or a post-execution alteration as an officer or other Minister or authorised person, is deemed to be the person who is entitled to sign⁷. Identical provisions apply to self-proving status and alterations⁸.

1 Sch 2, para 6.
2 See para 4.02.

3 Sch 2, para 6(1)(a).
4 Sch 2, para 6(1)(b).
5 Sch 2, para 6(1)(c).
6 Sch 2, para 6(1)(d).
7 Sch 2, para 6(2).
8 Sch 2, para 6(4), (6), (7).

CHAPTER 5

Repeals and amendments

Introduction

5.01 It is not the intention of this chapter to mention every repeal or every amendment, but we hope it will be helpful to identify a few which are of particular significance.

Repeals

5.02 As already mentioned, several Acts of the Scottish Parliament which dealt with the execution of deeds are repealed in whole. These are the Subscription of Deeds Acts 1540, 1579 and 1681. Also repealed are the Deeds Act 1696 and the Blank Bonds and Trusts Act 1696. The latter deals not only with blanks in deeds, but also proof of trusts. Among the sections of Acts which are repealed is section 6 of the Mercantile Law Amendment Act (Scotland) 1856, which gave rise to some doubt about the form required for the constitution of cautionary obligations. The following are also repealed: the Titles to Land Consolidation (Scotland) Act 1868, s 149, which dealt with partly printed deeds; and the Conveyancing (Scotland) Act 1874, ss 38–41, which dealt with witnessing of deeds, informalities of execution, the proof of holograph writings and notarial execution[1]. In connection with the latter, section 18 of and Schedule 1 to the Conveyancing (Scotland) Act 1924 are repealed, as is the Church of Scotland Property and Endowments Amendment Act 1933, s 13. The Conveyancing and Feudal Reform (Scotland) Act 1970, s 44, which simplified the previous system by providing that deeds, other than testamentary deeds, need be signed only on the last page is also repealed. The Prescription and Limitation (Scotland) Act 1973, Schedule 1, paragraph 2, provided that an obligation which was constituted by probative writ prescribed in 20 years and not 5. That provision is repealed, but it should be noted that obligations relating to land[2] are still governed by the 20-year prescription[3]. Other references to probative documents are repealed[4].

1 A consequential repeal is of the related provision in the Prescription and Limitation (Scotland) Act 1973, s 5.
2 1973 Act, Sch 1, para 2(e).
3 *Barratt (Scotland) Ltd v Keith* 1994 SLT 1337 and 1343.
4 1973 Act, Sch 1, paras 3 and 4(b).

Amendments

5.03 A general amendment of the 1995 Act is to statutes or other enactments which mention probativity, or probative deeds, or attested deeds. These are to be read as referring to the provisions of s 6(2) of the Act – the self-proving provisions. Examples are to be found in the Patents Act 1977[1] and the Housing (Scotland) Act 1987[2]. In enactments which have provisions for testing clauses[3] there is substituted a reference to the 1995 Act and the fact that a signature is all that is required for formal validity, but that witnessing may be desirable or essential for other purposes.

1 s 31(6).
2 s 53(1) and 54(6).
3 Eg Lands Clauses Consolidation (Scotland) Act 1845; Registration of Leases (Scotland) Act 1857; Transmission of Moveable Property (Scotland) Act 1862; Titles to Land Consolidation (Scotland) Act 1868; Conveyancing (Scotland) Act 1874; Trusts (Scotland) Act 1921; Conveyancing (Scotland) Act 1924; Succession (Scotland) Act 1964; Conveyancing and Feudal Reform (Scotland) Act 1970.

5.04 Two sets of changes which merit special attention are those relating to (a) succession and (b) companies.

(a) Succession

5.05 The Succession (Scotland) Act 1964, s 21 deals with evidence of testamentary writings in connection with the obtaining of confirmation. Section 21A is added by the 1995 Act and it provides that where the formal validity of the document is governed by Scots law confirmation is not granted unless the document is presumed to have been subscribed by the granter, either because it is witnessed (s 3) or because a court has made a finding to that effect (s 4). Because s 21 remains it is still necessary in the case of a holograph testamentary document to have affidavits from two witnesses regarding the handwriting and the signature of the testator.

Where the formal validity of the document is not governed by Scots law, the court must be satisfied that the document is formally valid according to the law governing that validity. Section 32 of the 1964 Act provided that a testamentary document which was not already 'probative' was to be treated as such if confirmation was obtained in Scotland to property disposed of in the document. The term 'probative' was not defined, but it would seem that it was intended to be the equivalent of 'validly executed'. The provision applied also if 'probate, letters of administration, or other grant of representation' was issued in England and Wales or Northern Ireland in respect of property disposed of in the document. The object of the provision was to render unnecessary all inquiry into the formal validity of a will as a link in title. The 1995 Act preserves the principle, but a new s 32 is substituted. The substitution provides that a document is formally valid if confirmation etc has been issued. The new provision, like the former one, is concerned only with formal validity and provides that the section does not prevent a challenge of the testamentary document on the ground that it is a forgery, or is not essentially valid (Sch 4, paras 38–40).

(b) Companies

5.06 Apart from the provisions about the execution of deeds by companies and self-proving status noted in Chapter 4[1], there are a number of changes to the Companies Act 1985 which are necessitated by the fact that companies no longer require to have common seals. Thus, the power given to a company to have a seal for use abroad is properly exercised if, instead of having the seal, the deed is executed in accordance with the 1995 Act[2]. The same provision is applied to share certificates[3], certificates evidencing shareholdings[4], and the issue and effect of share warrants payable to the bearer[5]. In the Insolvency Act 1986, s 53, which deals with the mode of appointment of a receiver by the holder of a floating charge, the 1995 Act provides that this appointment may be made by an instrument executed in accordance with the 1995 Act[6].

We have drawn attention to the most important repeals and amendments, but the full list of repeals is contained in Schedule 5 and amendments in Schedule 4 to the Act.

1 Companies Act 1985. See para 4.03.
2 Companies Act 1985, s 39(3), amended by the 1995 Act, Sch 4, para 53.
3 Companies Act 1985, s 40(2), inserted by the 1995 Act, Sch 4, para 54.
4 Companies Act 1985, s 186(2), inserted by the 1995 Act, Sch 4, para 55.
5 Companies Act 1985, s 188(2), amended by the 1995 Act, Sch 4, para 56.
6 Insolvency Act 1986, s 53, amended by the 1995 Act, Sch 4, para 58.

Appendices

Appendix 1: Subscription of Deeds Act 1540 (c 117)

Appendix 2: Subscription of Deeds Act 1579 (c 80)

Appendix 3: Subscription of Deeds Act 1681 (c 5)

Appendix 4: Deeds Act 1696 (c 15)

Appendix 5: Conveyancing (Scotland) Act 1874 (c 94), ss 38, 39

Appendix 6: Conveyancing and Feudal Reform (Scotland) Act 1970 (c 35), s 44

Appendix 7: Requirements of Writing (Scotland) Act 1995 (c 7)

APPENDIX 1

CAP. 37.

[1540, *cap.* 117.]

THAT na faith be gevin to euidentis selit without subscripcioun
be the principale or notare

ITEM It is statute and Ordanit that becaus mennys selis may of
aventure be tint quhairthrow grett hurt may be generit to
thaime that aw the samin And that mennis selis may be fenyeit
or putt to writtingis eftir thair deceise in hurt and preiudice of
our souerane lordis liegis That therefor na faith be gevin in
tyme cuming to ony obligatioune band or vther writting vnder
ane sele without subscriptioune of him that aw the samin and
witnesse Or ellis gif the party can nocht write with the subscriptioune of ane notar thairto

APPENDIX 2

CAP. 18.
[1579, *cap.* 80.]
ANENT the inserting of witnesses in obligationis and writtis of importance

ITEM it is statut and ordanit be oure souerane lord with auise of his thrie estaitis in parliament That all contractis obligationes reuersiones assignationes and discharges of reuersiones or eikis thairto And generalie all writtis importing heritable title or vtheris bandis and obligationes of greit importance to be maid in tyme cuming salbe subscriuit . . . be the principall pairtijs gif they can subscriue vtherwayis be twa famous notaris befoir foure famous witnesses denominat be thair speciall duelling places or sum vther euident takens That the witnesses be knawin be present at that tyme Otherwyse the saidis writtis to mak na fayth

APPENDIX 3

CAP. 5.
[1681, *cap.* 5.]

Act concerning probative witnesses in writs and Executions

OUR Soveraigne Lord Considering that by the Custome introduced when writing was not so ordinary Witnesses insert in
Writes although not subscryving are probative witnesses And
by their forgetfulnes may easily dissowne ther being
witnesses For remeid wherof His Majestie with advice and
Consent of the Estates of Parliament Doeth enact and Declare
that only subscribing Witnesses in writes to be subscribed by
any partie hereafter shall be probative and not the witnesses
insert not Subscribing And that all such writes to be subscribed heirafter wherin the Writer and witnesses are not
designed shall be null And are not supplyable by condescending vpon the Writer or the designation of the writer and
Witnesses And it is farder Statute and Declared that no witnes
shall subscribe as witnes to any parties subscription Unless he
then know that party and saw him Subscribe or saw or heard
him give Warrand to a Nottar or Nottars to subscribe for him
And in evidence thereof touch the Notars pen Or that the
party did at the time of the witnesses subscribing acknowledge his subscription Otherways the saids witnesses shall be
repute and punished as accessorie to forgerie And Seing Writting is now so ordinary His Majesty with consent foirsaid
Doeth enact and Declare that no witnesses But subscribing
witnesses shall be probative in Instruments of Sasine Instruments of Resignation Ad remanentiam Instruments of Intimation of Assignations Translations or Retrocessions to Bands
Contracts or other writs which shall happen to be subscribed in
any tyme heirafter And that none but subscryving witnesses
shall be probative in Executions of Messingers of Inhibitions of
Interdictions Hornings or Arrestment And that no Execution
whatsoever to be given hereafter shall be sufficient to infer

Interruption of Prescription in real Rights Unles the same be done before witnesses present at the doing thereof subscribing And that in all the saids caices The witnesses be designed in the body of the write Instrument or Execution respective Otherways the same shall be null and void And make no faith in Judgement nor outwith

APPENDIX 4

CAP. 15.
[1696, *cap.* 15.]
Act allowing Securities &c. to be written book wayes

OUR Soveraigne Lord understanding the great trouble and inconveniency the Leidges are put to in finding out of clauses and passages in long Contracts Decreits Dispositions Extracts Transumpts and other Securities consisting of many sheets battered togither which must be either folded or rolled togither Doth for remeid thereof with advice and consent of the Estates of Parliament Statute and Ordain that it shall be free hereafter for any person who hath any Contract Decreit Disposition or other Security above mentioned to write to choose whither he will have the same written in Sheets battered togither as formerly or to have them written by way of book in Leafs of Paper either in folio or quarto Provideing that if they be written bookways every page be marked by the number first second &c. and Signed as the margines were before and that the end of the last page make mention how many pages are therin contained in which page only witnesses are to signe in writts and Securities where witnesses are required by Law And which writts and Securities being written bookwayes marked and signed as said is His Majestie with consent forsaid declares to be als valid and formall as if they were written on severall Sheets battered togither and signed on the margine according to the present custome

Chapter 94

An Act to amend the Law relating to Land Rights and Conveyancing, and to facilitate the Transfer of Land, in Scotland — [7th August 1874]

38. Certain rules as to probative deeds altered

It shall be no objection to the probative character of a deed, instrument, or writing, whether relating to land or not, that the writer or printer is not named or designed, or that the number of pages is not specified, or that the witnesses are not named or designed in the body of such deed, instrument, or writing, or in the testing clause thereof, provided that where the witnesses are not so named and designed their designations shall be appended to or follow their subscriptions; and such designations may be so appended or added at any time before the deed, instrument, or writing shall have been recorded in any register for preservation, or shall have been founded on in any court, and need not be written by the witnesses themselves.

39. Deed not to be invalid because improbative

No deed, instrument, or writing subscribed by the granter or maker thereof, and bearing to be attested by two witnesses subscribing, and whether relating to land or not, shall be deemed invalid or denied effect according to its legal import because of any informality of execution, but the burden of proving that such deed, instrument, or writing so attested was subscribed by the granter or maker thereof, and by the witnesses by whom such deed, instrument, or writing bears to be attested, shall lie upon the party using or upholding the same, and such proof may be led in any action or proceeding in which such deed, instrument, or writing is founded on or objected to, or in a special application to the Court of Session, or to the sheriff within whose jurisdiction the defender in any such application resides, to have it declared that such deed, instrument, or writing was subscribed by such granter or maker and witnesses.

Conveyancing and Feudal Reform (Scotland) Act 1970

(1970 c 35)

44. Alteration of rules as to probative deeds

(1) Subject to the provisions of subsection (2) of this section, where—

(a) a conveyance, deed, instrument or writing, whether relating to land or not;

(b) an inventory, appendix, schedule, plan or other document annexed to such a conveyance, deed, instrument or writing,

is subscribed and (where appropriate) sealed on the last page, it shall be no objection to its probative character that it is not subscribed or, as the case may be, subscribed and sealed on every other page.

(2) Nothing in subsection (1) of this section shall affect the law relating to wills or other testamentary writings.

Requirements of Writing (Scotland) Act 1995 (c 7)

ARRANGEMENT OF SECTIONS

Section
1. Writing required for certain contracts, obligations, trusts, conveyances and wills.
2. Type of writing required for formal validity of certain documents.
3. Presumption as to granter's subscription or date or place of subscription.
4. Presumption as to granter's subscription or date or place of subscription when established in court proceedings.
5. Alterations to documents: formal validity and presumptions.
6. Registration of documents.
7. Subscription and signing.
8. Annexations to documents.
9. Subscription on behalf of blind granter or granter unable to write.
10. Forms of testing clause.
11. Abolition of proof by writ or oath, reference to oath and other common law rules.
12. Interpretation.
13. Application of Act to Crown.
14. Minor and consequential amendments, repeals, transitional provisions and savings.
15. Short title, commencement and extent.

SCHEDULES:
Schedule 1 — Alterations Made to a Document After it has been Subscribed.
Schedule 2 — Subscription and Signing: Special Cases.
Schedule 3 — Modifications of This Act in Relation to Subscription or Signing by Relevant Person under Section 9.
Schedule 4 — Minor and Consequential Amendments.
Schedule 5 — Repeals.

1. Writing required for certain contracts, obligations, trusts, conveyances and wills

(1) Subject to subsection (2) below and any other enactment, writing shall not be required for the constitution of a contract, unilateral obligation or trust.

(2) Subject to subsection (3) below, a written document complying with section 2 of this Act shall be required for—
   (a) the constitution of—
      (i) a contract or unilateral obligation for the creation, transfer, variation or extinction of an interest in land;
      (ii) a gratuitous unilateral obligation except an obligation undertaken in the course of business; and
      (iii) a trust whereby a person declares himself to be sole trustee of his own property or any property which he may acquire;
   (b) the creation, transfer, variation or extinction of an interest in land otherwise than by the operation of a court decree, enactment or rule of law; and
   (c) the making of any will, testamentary trust disposition and settlement or codicil.

(3) Where a contract, obligation or trust mentioned in subsection (2)(a) above is not constituted in a written document complying with section 2 of this Act, but one of the parties to the contract, a creditor in the obligation or a beneficiary under the trust ('the first person') has acted or refrained from acting in reliance on the contract, obligation or trust with the knowledge and acquiescence of the other party to the contract, the debtor in the obligation or the truster ('the second person')—
   (a) the second person shall not be entitled to withdraw from the contract, obligation or trust; and
   (b) the contract, obligation or trust shall not be regarded as invalid,
on the ground that it is not so constituted, if the condition set out in subsection (4) below is satisfied.

(4) The condition referred to in subsection (3) above is that the position of the first person—
   (a) as a result of acting or refraining from acting as mentioned in that subsection has been affected to a material extent; and
   (b) as a result of such a withdrawal as is mentioned in that subsection would be adversely affected to a material extent.

(5) In relation to the constitution of any contract, obligation or trust mentioned in subsection (2)(a) above, subsections (3) and (4) above replace the rules of law known as *rei interventus* and homologation.

(6) This section shall apply to the variation of a contract, obligation or trust as it applies to the constitution thereof but as if in subsections (3) and (4) for the references to acting or refraining from acting in reliance on the contract, obligation or trust and withdrawing therefrom there were substituted respectively references to acting or refraining from acting in reliance on the variation of the contract, obligation or trust and withdrawing from the variation.

(7) In this section 'interest in land' means any estate, interest or right in or over land, including any right to occupy or to use land or to restrict the occupation or use of land, but does not include—
(a) a tenancy;
(b) a right to occupy or use land; or
(c) a right to restrict the occupation or use of land,
if the tenancy or right is not granted for more than one year, unless the tenancy or right is for a recurring period or recurring periods and there is a gap of more than one year between the beginning of the first, and the end of the last, such period.

(8) For the purposes of subsection (7) above 'land' does not include—
(a) growing crops; or
(b) a moveable building or other moveable structure.

2. Type of writing required for formal validity of certain documents

(1) No document required by section 1(2) of this Act shall be valid in respect of the formalities of execution unless it is subscribed by the granter of it or, if there is more than one granter, by each granter, but nothing apart from such subscription shall be required for the document to be valid as aforesaid.

(2) A contract mentioned in section 1(2)(a)(i) of this Act may be regarded as constituted or varied (as the case may be) if the offer is contained in one or more documents and the acceptance is contained in another document or other documents, and each document is subscribed by the granter or granters thereof.

(3) Nothing in this section shall prevent a document which has not been subscribed by the granter or granters of it from being used as evidence in relation to any right or obligation to which the document relates.

(4) This section is without prejudice to any other enactment which makes different provision in respect of the formalities of execution of a document to which this section applies.

3. Presumption as to granter's subscription or date or place of subscription

(1) Subject to subsections (2) to (7) below, where—
    (a) a document bears to have been subscribed by a granter of it;
    (b) the document bears to have been signed by a person as a witness of that granter's subscription and the document, or the testing clause or its equivalent, bears to state the name and address of the witness; and
    (c) nothing in the document, or in the testing clause or its equivalent indicates—
        (i) that it was not subscribed by that granter as it bears to have been so subscribed; or
        (ii) that it was not validly witnessed for any reason specified in paragraphs (a) to (e) of subsection (4) below,
the document shall be presumed to have been subscribed by that granter.

(2) Where a testamentary document consists of more than one sheet, it shall not be presumed to have been subscribed by a granter as mentioned in subsection (1) above unless, in addition to it bearing to have been subscribed by him and otherwise complying with that subsection, it bears to have been signed by him on every sheet.

(3) For the purposes of subsection (1)(b) above—
    (a) the name and address of a witness may be added at any time before the document is—
        (i) founded on in legal proceedings; or
        (ii) registered for preservation in the Books of Council and Session or in sheriff court books; and
    (b) the name and address of a witness need not be written by the witness himself.

(4) Where, in any proceedings relating to a document in which a question arises as to a granter's subscription, it is established—

(a) that a signature bearing to be the signature of the witness of that granter's subscription is not such a signature, whether by reason of forgery or otherwise;

(b) that the person who signed the document as the witness of that granter's subscription is a person who is named in the document as a granter of it;

(c) that the person who signed the document as the witness of that granter's subscription, at the time of signing—

   (i)   did not know the granter;

   (ii) was under the age of 16 years; or

   (iii) was mentally incapable of acting as a witness;

(d) that the person who signed the document, purporting to be the witness of that granter's subscription, did not witness such subscription;

(e) that the person who signed the document as the witness of that granter's subscription did not sign the document after him or that the granter's subscription or, as the case may be, acknowledgement of his subscription and the person's signature as witness of that subscription were not one continuous process;

(f) that the name or address of the witness of that granter's subscription was added after the document was founded on or registered as mentioned in subsection (3)(a) above or is erroneous in any material respect; or

(g) in the case of a testamentary document consisting of more than one sheet, that a signature on any sheet bearing to be the signature of the granter is not such a signature, whether by reason of forgery or otherwise,

then, for the purposes of those proceedings, there shall be no presumption that the document has been subscribed by that granter.

(5) For the purposes of subsection (4)(c)(i) above, the witness shall be regarded as having known the person whose subscription he has witnessed at the time of witnessing if he had credible information at that time of his identity.

(6) For the purposes of subsection (4)(e) above, where—

(a) a document is granted by more than one granter; and

(b) a person is the witness to the subscription of more than one granter,

the subscription or acknowledgement of any such granter and the signature of the person witnessing that granter's subscription shall not be regarded as not being one continuous process by reason only that, between the time of that subscription or acknowledgement and that signature,

another granter has subscribed the document or acknowledged his subscription.

(7) For the purposes of the foregoing provisions of this
section a person witnesses a granter's subscription of a
document—

(a) if he sees the granter subscribe it; or
(b) if the granter acknowledges his subscription to that
person.

(8) Where—

(a) by virtue of subsection (1) above a document to which
this subsection applies is presumed to have been
subscribed by a granter of it;
(b) the document, or the testing clause or its equivalent,
bears to state the date or place of subscription of the
document by that granter; and
(c) nothing in the document, or in the testing clause or its
equivalent, indicates that that statement as to date or
place is incorrect,

there shall be a presumption that the document was subscribed by that granter on the date or at the place as stated.

(9) Subsection (8) above applies to any document other than a
testamentary document.

(10) Where—

(a) a testamentary document bears to have been subscribed and the document, or the testing clause or its
equivalent, bears to state the date or place of subscription (whether or not it is presumed under subsections
(1) to (7) above to have been subscribed by a granter of
it); and
(b) nothing in the document, or in the testing clause or its
equivalent, indicates that that statement as to date or
place is incorrect,

there shall be a presumption that the statement as to date
or place is correct.

4. Presumption as to granter's subscription or date or place of subscription when established in court proceedings

(1) Where a document bears to have been subscribed by a
granter of it, but there is no presumption under section 3 of
this Act that the document has been subscribed by that
granter, then, if the court, on an application being made to
it by any person who has an interest in the document, is
satisfied that the document was subscribed by that granter,
it shall—

(a) cause the document to be endorsed with a certificate to that effect; or

(b) where the document has already been registered in the Books of Council and Session or in sheriff court books, grant decree to that effect.

(2) Where a document bears to have been subscribed by a granter of it, but there is no presumption under section 3 of this Act as to the date or place of subscription, then, if the court, on an application being made to it by any person who has an interest in the document, is satisfied as to the date or place of subscription, it shall—

(a) cause the document to be endorsed with a certificate to that effect; or

(b) where the document has already been registered in the Books of Council and Session or in sheriff court books, grant decree to that effect.

(3) On an application under subsection (1) or (2) above evidence shall, unless the court otherwise directs, be given by affidavit.

(4) An application under subsection (1) or (2) above may be made either as a summary application or as incidental to and in the course of other proceedings.

(5) The effect of a certificate or decree—

(a) under subsection (1) above shall be to establish a presumption that the document has been subscribed by the granter concerned;

(b) under subsection (2) above shall be to establish a presumption that the statement in the certificate or decree as to date or place is correct.

(6) In this section 'the court' means—

(a) in the case of a summary application—

(i) the sheriff in whose sheriffdom the applicant resides; or

(ii) if the applicant does not reside in Scotland, the sheriff at Edinburgh; and

(b) in the case of an application made in the course of other proceedings, the court before which those proceedings are pending.

5. Alterations to documents: formal validity and presumptions

(1) An alteration made to a document required by section 1(2) of this Act—

    (a) before the document is subscribed by the granter or, if there is more than one granter, by the granter first subscribing it, shall form part of the document as so subscribed;

    (b) after the document is so subscribed shall, if the alteration has been signed by the granter or (as the case may be) by all the granters, have effect as a formally valid alteration of the document as so subscribed,

but an alteration made to such a document otherwise than as mentioned in paragraphs (a) and (b) above shall not be formally valid.

(2) Subsection (1) above is without prejudice to—

    (a) any rule of law enabling any provision in a testamentary document to be revoked by deletion or erasure without authentication of the deletion or erasure by the testator;

    (b) the Erasures in Deeds (Scotland) Act 1836 and section 54 of the Conveyancing (Scotland) Act 1874.

(3) The fact that an alteration to a document was made before the document was subscribed by the granter of it, or by the granter first subscribing it, may be established by all relevant evidence, whether written or oral.

(4) Where a document bears to have been subscribed by the granter or, if there is more than one granter, by all the granters of it, then, if subsection (5) or (6) below applies, an alteration made to the document shall be presumed to have been made before the document was subscribed by the granter or, if there is more than one granter, by the granter first subscribing it, and to form part of the document as so subscribed.

(5) This subsection applies where—

    (a) the document is presumed under section 3 of this Act to have been subscribed by the granter or granters (as the case may be);

    (b) it is stated in the document, or in the testing clause or its equivalent, that the alteration was made before the document was subscribed; and

    (c) nothing in the document, or in the testing clause or its equivalent, indicates that the alteration was made after the document was subscribed.

(6) This subsection applies where subsection (5) above does not apply, but the court is satisfied, on an application being made to it, that the alteration was made before the document was subscribed by the granter or, if there is more than one granter, by the granter first subscribing it, and causes

the document to be endorsed with a certificate to that effect or, where the document has already been registered in the Books of Council and Session or in sheriff court books, grants decree to that effect.

(7) Subsections (3), (4) and (6) of section 4 of this Act shall apply in relation to an application under subsection (6) above as they apply in relation to an application under subsection (1) of that section.

(8) Where an alteration is made to a document after the document has been subscribed by a granter, Schedule 1 to this Act (presumptions as to granter's signature and date and place of signing in relation to such alterations) shall have effect.

6. Registration of documents

(1) Subject to subsection (3) below, it shall not be competent—
   (a) to record a document in the Register of Sasines; or
   (b) to register a document for execution or preservation in the Books of Council and Session or in sheriff court books,
   unless subsection (2) below applies in relation to the document.

(2) This subsection applies where—
   (a) the document is presumed under section 3 or 4 of this Act to have been subscribed by the granter; or
   (b) if there is more than one granter, the document is presumed under section 3 or 4 or partly under the one section and partly under the other to have been subscribed by at least one of the granters.

(3) Subsection (1) above shall not apply in relation to—
   (a) the recording of a document in the Register of Sasines or the registration of a document in the Books of Council and Session or in sheriff court books, if such recording or registration is required or expressly permitted under any enactment;
   (b) the recording of a court decree in the Register of Sasines;
   (c) the registration in the Books of Council and Session or in sheriff court books of—
      (i) a testamentary document;
      (ii) a document which is directed by the Court of Session or (as the case may be) the sheriff to be so registered;

(iii) a document whose formal validity is governed by a law other than Scots law, if the Keeper of the Registers of Scotland or (as the case may be) the sheriff clerk is satisfied that the document is formally valid according to the law governing such validity;

(iv) a court decree granted under section 4 or 5 of this Act in relation to a document already registered in the Books of Council and Session or in sheriff court books (as the case may be); or

(d) the registration of a court decree in a separate register maintained for that purpose.

(4) A document may be registered for preservation in the Books of Council and Session or in sheriff court books without a clause of consent to registration.

7. Subscription and signing

(1) Except where an enactment expressly provides otherwise, a document is subscribed by a granter of it if it is signed by him at the end of the last page (excluding any annexation, whether or not incorporated in the document as provided for in section 8 of this Act).

(2) Subject to paragraph 2(2) of Schedule 2 to this Act, a document, or an alteration to a document, is signed by an individual natural person as a granter or on behalf of a granter of it if it is signed by him—

(a) with the full name by which he is identified in the document or in any testing clause or its equivalent; or

(b) with his surname, preceded by at least one forename (or an initial or abbreviation or familiar form of a forename); or

(c) except for the purposes of section 3(1) to (7) of this Act, with a name (not in accordance with paragraph (a) or (b) above) or description or an initial or mark if it is established that the name, description, initial or mark—

(i) was his usual method of signing, or his usual method of signing documents or alterations of the type in question; or

(ii) was intended by him as his signature of the document or alteration.

(3) Where there is more than one granter, the requirement under subsection (1) above of signing at the end of the last page of a document shall be regarded as complied with if at least one granter signs at the end of the last page and any other granter signs on an additional page.

(4) Where a person grants a document in more than one capacity, one subscription of the document by him shall be sufficient to bind him in all such capacities.

(5) A document, or an alteration to a document, is signed by a witness if it is signed by him—

    (a) with the full name by which he is identified in the document or in any testing clause or its equivalent; or

    (b) with his surname, preceded by at least one forename (or an initial or abbreviation or familiar form of a forename);

and if the witness is witnessing the signature of more than one granter, it shall be unnecessary for him to sign the document or alteration more than once.

(6) This section is without prejudice to any rule of law relating to the subscription or signing of documents by members of the Royal Family, by peers or by the wives of the eldest sons of peers.

(7) Schedule 2 to this Act (special rules relating to subscription and signing of documents etc by partnerships, companies, local authorities, other bodies corporate and Ministers) shall have effect.

8. Annexations to documents

(1) Subject to subsection (2) below and except where an enactment expressly otherwise provides, any annexation to a document shall be regarded as incorporated in the document if it is—

    (a) referred to in the document; and

    (b) identified on its face as being the annexation referred to in the document,

without the annexation having to be signed or subscribed.

(2) Where a document relates to land and an annexation to it describes or shows all or any part of the land to which the document relates, the annexation shall be regarded as incorporated in the document if and only if—

    (a) it is referred to in the document; and

    (b) it is identified on its face as being the annexation referred to in the document; and

    (c) it is signed on—

        (i) each page, where it is a plan, drawing, photograph or other representation; or

        (ii) the last page, where it is an inventory, appendix, schedule or other writing.

(3) Any annexation referred to in subsection (2) above which bears to have been signed by a granter of the document shall be presumed to have been signed by the person who subscribed the document as that granter.

(4) Section 7(2) of this Act shall apply in relation to any annexation referred to in subsection (2) above as it applies in relation to a document as if for any reference to a document (except the reference in paragraph (a)) there were substituted a reference to an annexation.

(5) It shall be competent to sign any annexation to a document at any time before the document is—

    (a) founded on in legal proceedings;

    (b) registered for preservation in the Books of Council and Session or in sheriff court books;

    (c) recorded in the Register of Sasines;

    (d) registered in the Land Register of Scotland.

(6) Where there is more than one granter, the requirement under subsection (2)(c)(ii) above of signing on the last page shall be regarded as complied with (provided that at least one granter signs at the end of the last page) if any other granter signs on an additional page.

9. Subscription on behalf of blind granter or granter unable to write

(1) Where a granter of a document makes a declaration to a relevant person that he is blind or unable to write, the relevant person—

    (a) having read the document to that granter; or

    (b) if the granter makes a declaration that he does not wish him to do so, without having read it to the granter,

shall, if authorised by the granter, be entitled to subscribe it and, if it is a testamentary document, sign it as mentioned in section 3(2) of this Act, on the granter's behalf.

(2) Subscription or signing by a relevant person under subsection (1) above shall take place in the presence of the granter.

(3) This Act shall have effect in relation to subscription or signing by a relevant person under subsection (1) above subject to the modifications set out in Schedule 3 to this Act.

(4) A document subscribed by a relevant person under subsection (1) above which confers on the relevant person or his spouse, son or daughter a benefit in money or money's worth (whether directly or indirectly) shall be invalid to the extent, but only to the extent, that it confers such benefit.

(5) This section and Schedule 3 to this Act apply in relation to the signing of—

    (a) an annexation to a document as mentioned in section 8(2) of this Act;

    (b) an alteration made to a document or to any such annexation to a document.

as they apply in relation to the subscription of a document; and for that purpose, any reference to reading a document includes a reference to describing a plan, drawing, photograph or other representation in such an annexation or in an alteration to such an annexation.

(6) In this Act 'relevant person' means a solicitor who has in force a practising certificate as defined in section 4(c) of the Solicitors (Scotland) Act 1980, an advocate, a justice of the peace or a sheriff clerk and, in relation to the execution of documents outwith Scotland, includes a notary public or any other person with official authority under the law of the place of execution to execute documents on behalf of persons who are blind or unable to write.

(7) Nothing in this section shall prevent the granter of a document who is blind from subscribing or signing the document as mentioned in section 7 of this Act.

10. Forms of testing clause

(1) Without prejudice to the effectiveness of any other means of providing information relating to the excecution of a document, this information may be provided in such form of testing clause as may be prescribed in regulations made by the Secretary of State.

(2) Regulations under subsection (1) above shall be made by statutory instrument which shall be subject to annulment in pursuance of a resolution of either House of Parliament and may prescribe different forms for different cases or classes of case.

11. Abolition of proof by writ or oath, reference to oath and other common law rules

(1) Any rule of law and any enactment whereby the proof of any matter is restricted to proof by writ or by reference to oath shall cease to have effect.

(2) The procedure of proving any matter in any civil proceedings by reference to oath is hereby abolished.

(3) The following rules of law shall cease to have effect—

(a) any rule whereby certain contracts and obligations and any variations of those contracts and obligations, and assignations of incorporeal moveables, are required to be in writing; and

(b) any rule which confers any privilege—
  (i) on a document which is holograph or adopted as holograph; or
  (ii) on a writ *in re mercatoria*.

(4) Subsections (1) and (2) above shall not apply in relation to proceedings commenced before the commencement of this Act.

12. Interpretation

(1) In this Act, except where the context otherwise requires—
  'alteration' includes interlineation, marginal addition, deletion, substitution, erasure or anything written on erasure;

  'annexation' includes any inventory, appendix, schedule, other writing, plan, drawing, photograph or other representation annexed to a document;

  'authorised' means expressly or impliedly authorised and any reference to a person authorised to sign includes a reference to a person authorised to sign generally or in relation to a particular document;

  'company' has the same meaning as in section 735(1) of the Companies Act 1985;

  'decree' includes a judgment or order, or an official certified copy, abbreviate or extract of a decree;

  'director' includes any person occupying the position of director, by whatever name he is called;

  'document' includes any annexation which is incorporated in it under section 8 of this Act and any reference, however expressed, to the signing of a document includes a reference to the signing of an annexation;

  'enactment' includes an enactment contained in a statutory instrument;

  'governing board', in relation to a body corporate to which paragraph 5 of Schedule 2 to this Act applies, means any governing body, however described;

  'local authority' means a local authority within the meaning of section 235(1) of the Local Government (Scotland) Act 1973 and a council constituted under section 2 of the Local Government etc. (Scotland) Act 1994;

'Minister' has the same meaning as 'Minister of the Crown' has in section 8 of the Ministers of the Crown Act 1975;

'office-holder' does not include a Minister but, subject to that, means—

(a) the holder of an office created or continued in existence by a public general Act of Parliament;

(b) the holder of an office the remuneration in respect of which is paid out of money provided by Parliament; and

(c) the registrar of companies within the meaning of the Companies Act 1985;

'officer'—

(a) in relation to a Minister, means any person in the civil service of the Crown who is serving in his Department;

(b) in relation to an office-holder, means any member of his staff, or any person in the civil service of the Crown who has been assigned or appointed to assist him in the exercise of his functions;

'proper officer', in relation to a local authority, has the same meaning as in section 235(3) of the Local Government (Scotland) Act 1973; and

'secretary' means, if there are two or more joint secretaries, any one of them.

(2) Any reference in this Act to subscription or signing by a granter of a document or an alteration made to a document, in a case where a person is subscribing or signing under a power of attorney on behalf of the granter, shall be construed as a reference to subscription or signing by that person of the document or alteration.

13. Application of Act to Crown

(1) Nothing in this Act shall—

(a) prevent Her Majesty from authenticating—

(i) a document by superscription; or

(ii) a document relating to her private estates situated or arising in Scotland in accordance with section 6 of the Crown Private Estates Act 1862;

(b) prevent authentication under the Writs Act 1672 of a document passing the seal appointed by the Treaty of Union to be kept and used in Scotland in place of the Great Seal of Scotland formerly in use; or

(c) prevent any document mentioned in paragraph (a) or (b) above authenticated as aforesaid from being recorded in the Register of Sasines or registered for execution or preservation in the Books of Council and Session or in sheriff court books.

(2) Nothing in this Act shall prevent a Crown writ from being authenticated or recorded in Chancery under section 78 of the Titles to Land Consolidation (Scotland) Act 1868.

(3) Subject to subsections (1) and (2) above, this Act binds the Crown.

14. Minor and consequential amendments, repeals, transitional provisions and savings

(1) The enactments mentioned in Schedule 4 to this Act shall have effect subject to the minor and consequential amendments specified in that Schedule.

(2) The enactments mentioned in Schedule 5 to this Act are hereby repealed to the extent specified in the third column of that Schedule.

(3) Subject to subsection (4) below and without prejudice to subsection (5) below and section 11(4) of this Act, nothing in this Act shall—

(a) apply to any document executed or anything done before the commencement of this Act; or

(b) affect the operation, in relation to any document executed before such commencement, of any procedure for establishing the authenticity of such a document.

(4) In the repeal of the Blank Bonds and Trusts Act 1696 (provided for in Schedule 5 to this Act), the repeal of the words 'And farder' to the end—

(a) shall have effect in relation to a deed of trust, whether executed before or after the commencement of this Act; but

(b) notwithstanding paragraph (a) above, shall not have effect in relation to proceedings commenced before the commencement of this Act in which a question arises as to the deed of trust.

(5) The repeal of certain provisions of the Lyon King of Arms Act 1672 (provided for in Schedule 5 to this Act) shall not affect any right of a person to add a territorial designation to his signature or the jurisdiction of the Lord Lyon King of Arms in relation to any such designation.

(6) For the purposes of this Act, if it cannot be ascertained whether a document was executed before or after the commencement of this Act, there shall be a presumption that it was executed after such commencement.

15. Short title, commencement and extent

(1) This Act may be cited as the Requirements of Writing (Scotland) Act 1995.

(2) This Act shall come into force at the end of the period of three months beginning with the date on which it is passed.

(3) This Act extends to Scotland only.

SCHEDULES

SCHEDULE 1

ALTERATIONS MADE TO A DOCUMENT AFTER IT HAS BEEN SUBSCRIBED

Presumption as to granter's signature or date or place of signing

1.—(1) Subject to sub-paragraphs (2) to (7) below, where—
   (a) an alteration to a document bears to have been signed by a granter of the document;
   (b) the alteration bears to have been signed by a person as a witness of that granter's signature and the alteration, or the testing clause or its equivalent, bears to state the name and address of the witness; and
   (c) nothing in the document or alteration, or in the testing clause or its equivalent, indicates—
      (i) that the alteration was not signed by that granter as it bears to have been so signed; or
      (ii) that it was not validly witnessed for any reason specified in paragraphs (a) to (e) of sub-paragraph (4) below,
   the alteration shall be presumed to have been signed by that granter.

   (2) Where an alteration to a testamentary document consists of more than one sheet, the alteration shall not be presumed to have been signed by a granter as mentioned in sub-paragraph (1) above unless, in addition to it bearing to have been signed by him on the last sheet and otherwise complying with that sub-paragraph, it bears to have been signed by him on every other sheet.

   (3) For the purposes of sub-paragraph (1)(b) above—
      (a) the name and address of a witness may be added at any time before the alteration is—
         (i) founded on in legal proceedings; or

      (ii) registered for preservation in the Books of Council and Session or in sheriff court books; and

  (b) the name and address of a witness need not be written by the witness himself.

(4) Where, in any proceedings relating to an alteration to a document in which a question arises as to a granter's signature, it is established—

  (a) that a signature bearing to be the signature of the witness of that granter's signature is not such a signature, whether by reason of forgery or otherwise;

  (b) that the person who signed the alteration as the witness of that granter's signature is a person who is named in the document as a granter of the document;

  (c) that the person who signed the alteration as the witness of that granter's signature, at the time of signing—

    (i)   did not know the granter;

    (ii) was under the age of 16 years; or

    (iii) was mentally incapable of acting as a witness;

  (d) that the person who signed the alteration, purporting to be the witness of that granter's signature, did not witness such signature;

  (e) that the person who signed the alteration as the witness of that granter's signature did not sign the alteration after him or that the signing of the alteration by the granter or, as the case may be, the granter's acknowledgement of his signature and the signing by the person as witness were not one continuous process;

  (f) that the name or address of the witness of that granter's signature was added after the alteration was founded on or registered as mentioned in sub-paragraph (3)(a) above or is erroneous in any material respect; or

  (g) in the case of an alteration to a testamentary document consisting of more than one sheet, that a signature on any sheet of the alteration bearing to be the signature of the granter is not such a signature, whether by reason of forgery or otherwise,

then, for the purposes of those proceedings, there shall be no presumption that the alteration has been signed by that granter.

(5) For the purposes of sub-paragraph (4)(c)(i) above, the witness shall be regarded as having known the person whose signature he has witnessed at the time of witnessing if he had credible information at that time of his identity.

(6) For the purposes of sub-paragraph (4)(e) above, where—

  (a) an alteration to a document is made by more than one granter; and

  (b) a person is the witness to the signature of more than one granter;

the signing of the alteration by any such granter or the acknowledgement of his signature and the signing by the person witnessing that granter's signature shall not be regarded as not being one continuous process by reason only that, between the time of signing or acknowledgement by that granter and of signing by that witness, another granter has signed the alteration or acknowledged his signature.

(7) For the purposes of the foregoing provisions of this paragraph a person witnesses a granter's signature of an alteration—
   (a) if he sees the granter sign it; or
   (b) if the granter acknowledges his signature to that person.

(8) Where—
   (a) by virtue of sub-paragraph (1) above an alteration to a document to which this sub-paragraph applies is presumed to have been signed by a granter of the document;
   (b) the alteration, or the testing clause or its equivalent, bears to state the date or place of signing of the alteration by that granter; and
   (c) nothing in the document or alteration, or in the testing clause or its equivalent, indicates that that statement as to date or place is incorrect,
   there shall be a presumption that the alteration was signed by that granter on the date or at the place as stated.

(9) Sub-paragraph (8) above applies to any document other than a testamentary document.

(10) Where—
   (a) an alteration to a testamentary document bears to have been signed and the alteration, or the testing clause or its equivalent, bears to state the date or place of signing (whether or not it is presumed under sub-paragraphs (1) to (7) above to have been signed by a granter of the document); and
   (b) nothing in the document or alteration, or in the testing clause or its equivalent, indicates that that statement as to date or place is incorrect,
   there shall be a presumption that the statement as to date or place is correct.

Presumption as to granter's signature or date or place of signing when established in court proceedings

2.—(1) Where an alteration to a document bears to have been signed by a granter of the document, but there is no presumption under paragraph 1 above that the alteration has been signed by that granter, then, if the court, on an application being made to it by any person having an interest in the document, is satisfied that the alteration was signed by that granter, it shall—
   (a) cause the document to be endorsed with a certificate to that effect; or
   (b) where the document has already been registered in the Books of Council and Session or in sheriff court books, grant decree to that effect.

(2) Where an alteration to a document bears to have been signed by a granter of the document, but there is no presumption under paragraph 1 above as to the date or place of signing, then, if the court, on an application being made to it by any person having an interest in the document, is satisfied as to the date or place of signing, it shall—

    (a) cause the document to be endorsed with a certificate to that effect; or

    (b) where the document has already been registered in the Books of Council and Session or in sheriff court books, grant decree to that effect.

(3) In relation to an application under sub-paragraph (1) or (2) above evidence shall, unless the court otherwise directs, be given by affidavit.

(4) An application under sub-paragraph (1) or (2) above may be made either as a summary application or as incidental to and in the course of other proceedings.

(5) The effect of a certificate or decree—

    (a) under sub-paragraph (1) above shall be to establish a presumption that the alteration has been signed by the granter concerned;

    (b) under sub-paragraph (2) above shall be to establish a presumption that the statement in the certificate or decree as to date or place is correct.

(6) In this paragraph 'the court' means—

    (a) in the case of a summary application—

        (i) the sheriff in whose sheriffdom the applicant resides; or

        (ii) if the applicant does not reside in Scotland, the sheriff at Edinburgh; and

    (b) in the case of an application made in the course of other proceedings, the court before which those proceedings are pending.

SCHEDULE 2

SUBSCRIPTION AND SIGNING: SPECIAL CASES

General

1. Any reference in this Act to subscription or signing by a granter of a document or an alteration to a document, in a case where the granter is a person to whom any of paragraphs 2 to 6 of this Schedule applies shall, unless the context otherwise requires, be construed as a reference to subscription or, as the case may be, signing of the document or alteration by a person in accordance with that paragraph.

Partnerships

2.—(1) Except where an enactment expressly provides otherwise, where a granter of a document is a partnership, the document is signed by the partnership if it is signed on its behalf by a partner or by a person authorised to sign the document on its behalf.

(2) A person signing on behalf of a partnership under this paragraph may use his own name or the firm name.

(3) Sub-paragraphs (1) and (2) of this paragraph apply in relation to the signing of an alteration made to a document as they apply in relation to the signing of a document.

(4) In this paragraph 'partnership' has the same meaning as in section 1 of the Partnership Act 1890.

Companies

3.—(1) Except where an enactment expressly provides otherwise, where a granter of a document is a company, the document is signed by the company if it is signed on its behalf by a director, or by the secretary, of the company or by a person authorised to sign the document on its behalf.

(2) This Act is without prejudice to—

    (a) section 283(3) of the Companies Act 1985; and

    (b) paragraph 9 of Schedule 1, paragraph 9 of Schedule 2, and paragraph 7 of Schedule 4, to the Insolvency Act 1986.

(3) Sub-paragraphs (1) and (2) of this paragraph apply in relation to the signing of an alteration made to a document as they apply in relation to the signing of a document.

(4) Where a granter of a document is a company, section 3 of and Schedule 1 to this Act shall have effect subject to the modifications set out in sub-paragraphs (5) and (6) below.

(5) In section 3—

    (a) for subsection (1) there shall be substituted the following subsections—

        '(1) Subject to subsections (1A) to (7) below, where—

            (a) a document bears to have been subscribed on behalf of a company by a director, or by the secretary, of the company or by a person bearing to have been authorised to subscribe the document on its behalf;

            (b) the document bears to have been signed by a person as a witness of the subscription of the director, secretary or other person subscribing on behalf of the company and to state the name and address of the witness; and

            (c) nothing in the document, or in the testing clause or its equivalent, indicates—

                (i) that it was not subscribed on behalf of the company as it bears to have been so subscribed; or

                (ii) that it was not validly witnessed for any reason specified in paragraphs (a) to (e) of subsection (4) below,

the document shall be presumed to have been subscribed by the company.

    (1A) Where a document does not bear to have been signed by a person as a witness of the subscription of the director, secretary or other person subscribing on behalf of the company it shall be presumed to have been subscribed by the company if it bears to have been subscribed on behalf of the company by—

(a) two directors of the company; or

(b) a director and secretary of the company; or

(c) two persons bearing to have been authorised to subscribe the document on its behalf.

(1B) For the purposes of subsection (1)(b) above, the name and address of the witness may bear to be stated in the document itself or in the testing clause or its equivalent.

(1C) A presumption under subsection (1) or (1A) above as to subscription of a document does not include a presumption—

(a) that a person bearing to subscribe the document as a director or the secretary of the company was such director or secretary; or

(b) that a person subscribing the document on behalf of the company bearing to have been authorised to do so was authorised to do so.';

(b) in subsection (4) after paragraph (g) there shall be inserted the following paragraph—

'(h) if the document does not bear to have been witnessed, but bears to have been subscribed on behalf of the company by two of the directors of the company, or by a director and secretary of the company, or by two authorised persons, that a signature bearing to be the signature of a director, secretary or authorised person is not such a signature, whether by reason of forgery or otherwise;'.

(6) In paragraph 1 of Schedule 1—

(a) for sub-paragraph (1) there shall be substituted the following sub-paragraphs—

'(1) Subject to sub-paragraphs (1A) to (7) below, where—

(a) an alteration to a document bears to have been signed on behalf of a company by a director, or by the secretary, of the company or by a person bearing to have been authorised to sign the alteration on its behalf;

(b) the alteration bears to have been signed by a person as a witness of the signature of the director, secretary or other person signing on behalf of the company and to state the name and address of the witness; and

(c) nothing in the document or alteration, or in the testing clause or its equivalent, indicates—

(i) that the alteration was not signed on behalf of the company as it bears to have been so signed; or

(ii) that the alteration was not validly witnessed for any reason specified in paragraphs (a) to (e) of sub-paragraph (4) below,

the alteration shall be presumed to have been signed by the company.

(1A) Where an alteration does not bear to have been signed by a person as a witness of the signature of the director, secretary or other person signing on behalf of the company it shall be presumed to have been signed by the company if it bears to have been signed on behalf of the company by—

(a) two directors of the company; or

(b) a director and secretary of the company; or

(c) two persons bearing to have been authorised to sign the alteration on its behalf.

(1B) For the purposes of sub-paragraph (1)(b) above, the name and address of the witness may bear to be stated in the alteration itself or in the testing clause or its equivalent.

(1C) A presumption under sub-paragraph (1) or (1A) above as to signing of an alteration to a document does not include a presumption—

(a) that a person bearing to sign the alteration as a director or the secretary of the company was such director or secretary; or

(b) that a person signing the alteration on behalf of the company bearing to have been authorised to do so was authorised to do so.';

(b) in sub-paragraph (4) after paragraph (g) there shall be inserted the following paragraph—

'(h) if the alteration does not bear to have been witnessed, but bears to have been signed on behalf of the company by two of the directors of the company, or by a director and secretary of the company, or by two authorised persons, that a signature bearing to be the signature of a director, secretary or authorised person is not such a signature, whether by reason of forgery or otherwise;'.

Local authorities

4.—(1) Except where an enactment expressly provides otherwise, where a granter of a document is a local authority, the document is signed by the authority if it is signed on their behalf by the proper officer of the authority.

(2) For the purposes of the signing of a document under this paragraph, a person purporting to sign on behalf of a local authority as an officer of the authority shall be presumed to be the proper officer of the authority.

(3) Sub-paragraphs (1) and (2) of this paragraph apply in relation to the signing of an alteration made to a document as they apply in relation to the signing of a document.

(4) Where a granter of a document is a local authority, section 3 of and Schedule 1 to this Act shall have effect subject to the modifications set out in sub-paragraphs (5) to (8) below.

(5) For section 3(1) there shall be substituted the following subsections—

'(1) Subject to subsections (1A) to (7) below, where—

(a) a document bears to have been subscribed on behalf of a local authority by the proper officer of the authority;

(b) the document bears—
  (i) to have been signed by a person as a witness of the proper officer's subscription and to state the name and address of the witness; or
  (ii) (if the subscription is not so witnessed), to have been sealed with the common seal of the authority; and
(c) nothing in the document, or in the testing clause or its equivalent, indicates—
  (i) that it was not subscribed on behalf of the authority as it bears to have been so subscribed; or
  (ii) that it was not validly witnessed for any reason specified in paragraphs (a) to (e) of subsection (4) below or that it was not sealed as it bears to have been sealed or that it was not validly sealed for the reason specified in subsection (4)(h) below,

the document shall be presumed to have been subscribed by the proper officer and by the authority.

(1A) For the purposes of subsection (1)(b)(i) above, the name and address of the witness may bear to be stated in the document itself or in the testing clause or its equivalent.'.

(6) In section 3(4) after paragraph (g) there shall be inserted the following paragraph—

'(h) if the document does not bear to have been witnessed, but bears to have been sealed with the common seal of the authority, that it was sealed by a person without authority to do so or was not sealed on the date on which it was subscribed on behalf of the authority;'.

(7) For paragraph 1(1) of Schedule 1 there shall be substituted the following sub-paragraphs—

'(1) Subject to sub-paragraphs (1A) to (7) below, where—
(a) an alteration to a document bears to have been signed on behalf of a local authority by the proper officer of the authority;
(b) the alteration bears—
  (i) to have been signed by a person as a witness of the proper officer's signature and to state the name and address of the witness; or
  (ii) (if the signature is not so witnessed), to have been sealed with the common seal of the authority; and
(c) nothing in the document or alteration, or in the testing clause or its equivalent, indicates—
  (i) that the alteration was not signed on behalf of the authority as it bears to have been so signed; or
  (ii) that the alteration was not validly witnessed for any reason specified in paragraphs (a) to (e) of sub-paragraph (4) below or that it was not sealed as it bears to have been sealed or that it was not validly sealed for the reason specified in sub-paragraph (4)(h) below,

the alteration shall be presumed to have been signed by the proper officer and by the authority.

(1A) For the purposes of sub-paragraph (1)(b)(i) above, the name and address of the witness may bear to be stated in the alteration itself or in the testing clause or its equivalent.'.

(8) In paragraph 1(4) of Schedule 1 after paragraph (g) there shall be inserted the following paragraph—

'(h) if the alteration does not bear to have been witnessed, but bears to have been sealed with the common seal of the authority, that it was sealed by a person without authority to do so or was not sealed on the date on which it was signed on behalf of the authority;'.

Other bodies corporate

5.—(1) This paragraph applies to any body corporate other than a company or a local authority.

(2) Except where an enactment expressly provides otherwise, where a granter of a document is a body corporate to which this paragraph applies, the document is signed by the body if it is signed on its behalf by—

(a) a member of the body's governing board or, if there is no governing board, a member of the body;

(b) the secretary of the body by whatever name he is called; or

(c) a person authorised to sign the document on behalf of the body.

(3) Sub-paragraphs (1) and (2) of this paragraph apply in relation to the signing of an alteration made to a document as they apply in relation to the signing of a document.

(4) Where a granter of a document is a body corporate to which this paragraph applies, section 3 of and Schedule 1 to this Act shall have effect subject to the modifications set out in sub-paragraphs (5) to (8) below.

(5) For section 3(1) there shall be substituted the following subsections—

'(1) Subject to subsections (1A) to (7) below, where—

(a) a document bears to have been subscribed on behalf of a body corporate to which paragraph 5 of Schedule 2 to this Act applies by—

(i) a member of the body's governing board or, if there is no governing board, a member of the body;

(ii) the secretary of the body; or

(iii) a person bearing to have been authorised to subscribe the document on its behalf;

(b) the document bears—

(i) to have been signed by a person as a witness of the subscription of the member, secretary or other person signing on behalf of the body and to state the name and address of the witness; or

   (ii) (if the subscription is not so witnessed), to have been
    sealed with the common seal of the body; and
  (c) nothing in the document, or in the testing clause or its
   equivalent, indicates—
    (i) that it was not subscribed on behalf of the body as it
     bears to have been so subscribed; or
    (ii) that it was not validly witnessed for any reason
     specified in paragraphs (a) to (e) of subsection (4)
     below or that it was not sealed as it bears to have been
     sealed or that it was not validly sealed for the reason
     specified in subsection (4)(h) below,
the document shall be presumed to have been subscribed by the
member, secretary or authorised person (as the case may be) and
by the body.

 (1A) For the purposes of subsection (1)(b)(i) above, the name
and address of the witness may bear to be stated in the document
itself or in the testing clause or its equivalent.

 (1B) A presumption under subsection (1) above as to subscription of a document does not include a presumption—
 (a) that a person bearing to subscribe the document as a member
  of the body's governing board, a member of the body or the
  secretary of the body was such member or secretary; or
 (b) that a person subscribing the document on behalf of the body
  bearing to have been authorised to do so was authorised to do so.'.

(6) In section 3(4) after paragraph (g) there shall be inserted the following paragraph—
 '(h) if the document does not bear to have been witnessed, but
  bears to have been sealed with the common seal of the body,
  that it was sealed by a person without authority to do so or
  was not sealed on the date on which it was subscribed on
  behalf of the body;'.

(7) For paragraph 1(1) of Schedule 1 there shall be substituted the following sub-paragraphs—
 '(1) Subject to sub-paragraph (1A) to (7) below, where—
  (a) an alteration to a document bears to have been signed on
   behalf of a body corporate to which paragraph 5 of
   Schedule 2 to this Act applies by—
    (i) a member of the body's governing board or, if there is
     no governing board, a member of the body;
    (ii) the secretary of the body; or
    (iii) a person bearing to have been authorised to sign the
     alteration on its behalf;
  (b) the alteration bears—
    (i) to have been signed by a person as a witness of the
     signature of the member, secretary or other person
     signing on behalf of the body and to state the name and
     address of the witness; or
    (ii) (if the signature is not so witnessed), to have been
     sealed with the common seal of the body; and

(c) nothing in the document or alteration, or in the testing clause or its equivalent, indicates—
  (i) that the alteration was not signed on behalf of the body as it bears to have been so signed; or
  (ii) that the alteration was not validly witnessed for any reason specified in paragraphs (a) to (e) of sub-paragraph (4) below or that it was not sealed as it bears to have been sealed or that it was not validly sealed for the reason specified in sub-paragraph (4)(h) below,

the alteration shall be presumed to have been signed by the member, secretary or authorised person (as the case may be) and by the body.

(1A) For the purposes of sub-paragraph (1)(b)(i) above, the name and address of the witness may bear to be stated in the alteration itself or in the testing clause or its equivalent.

(1B) A presumption under sub-paragraph (1) above as to signing of an alteration to a document does not include a presumption—
(a) that a person bearing to sign the alteration as a member of the body's governing board, a member of the body or the secretary of the body was such member or secretary; or
(b) that a person signing the alteration on behalf of the body bearing to have been authorised to do so was authorised to do so.'.

(8) In paragraph 1(4) of Schedule 1 after paragraph (g) there shall be inserted the following paragraph—
'(h) if the alteration does not bear to have been witnessed, but bears to have been sealed with the common seal of the body, that it was sealed by a person without authority to do so or was not sealed on the date on which it was signed on behalf of the body;'.

Ministers of the Crown and office-holders

6.—(1) Except where an enactment expressly provides otherwise, where a granter of a document is a Minister or an office-holder, the document is signed by the Minister or office-holder if it is signed—
(a) by him personally; or
(b) in a case where by virtue of any enactment or rule of law a document by a Minister may be signed by an officer of his or by any other Minister, by that officer or by that other Minister as the case may be; or
(c) in a case where by virtue of any enactment or rule of law a document by an office-holder may be signed by an officer of his, by that officer; or
(d) by any other person authorised to sign the document on his behalf.

(2) For the purposes of the signing of a document under this paragraph, a person purporting to sign—

    (a) as an officer as mentioned in sub-paragraph (1)(b) or (1)(c) above;

    (b) as another Minister as mentioned in sub-paragraph (1)(b) above;

    (c) as a person authorised as mentioned in sub-paragraph (1)(d) above,

shall be presumed to be the officer, other Minister or authorised person, as the case may be.

(3) Sub-paragraphs (1) and (2) of this paragraph are without prejudice to section 3 of and Schedule 1 to the Ministers of the Crown Act 1975.

(4) Sub-paragraphs (1) to (3) of this paragraph apply in relation to the signing of an alteration made to a document as they apply in relation to the signing of a document.

(5) Where a granter of a document is a Minister or office-holder, section 3 of and Schedule 1 to this Act shall have effect subject to the modifications set out in sub-paragraphs (6) and (7) below.

(6) For section 3(1) there shall be substituted the following subsections—

'(1) Subject to subsections (1A) to (7) below, where—

    (a) a document bears to have been subscribed—

        (i) by a Minister or, in a case where by virtue of any enactment or rule of law a document by a Minister may be signed by an officer of his or by any other Minister, by that officer or by that other Minister; or

        (ii) by an office-holder or, in a case where by virtue of any enactment or rule of law a document by an office-holder may be signed by an officer of his, by that officer; or

        (iii) by any other person bearing to have been authorised to subscribe the document on behalf of the Minister or office-holder;

    (b) the document bears to have been signed by a person as a witness of the subscription mentioned in paragraph (a) above and to state the name and address of the witness; and

    (c) nothing in the document, or in the testing clause or its equivalent, indicates—

        (i) that it was not subscribed as it bears to have been subscribed; or

        (ii) that it was not validly witnessed for any reason specified in paragraphs (a) to (e) of subsection (4) below,

the document shall be presumed to have been subscribed by the officer, other Minister or authorised person and by the Minister or office-holder, as the case may be.

(1A) For the purposes of subsection (1)(b) above, the name and address of the witness may bear to be stated in the document itself or in the testing clause or its equivalent.'.

(7) For paragraph 1(1) of Schedule 1 there shall be substituted the following sub-paragraphs—

'(1) Subject to sub-paragraphs (1A) to (7) below, where—

    (a) an alteration to a document bears to have been signed by—

        (i) a Minister or, in a case where by virtue of any enactment or rule of law a document by a Minister may be signed by an officer of his or by any other Minister, by that officer or by that other Minister; or

        (ii) an office-holder or, in a case where by virtue of any enactment or rule of law a document by an office-holder may be signed by an officer of his, by that officer; or

        (iii) any other person bearing to have been authorised to sign the alteration on behalf of the Minister or office-holder;

    (b) the alteration bears to have been signed by a person as a witness of the signature mentioned in paragraph (a) above and to state the name and address of the witness; and

    (c) nothing in the document or alteration, or in the testing clause or its equivalent, indicates—

        (i) that the alteration was not signed as it bears to have been signed; or

        (ii) that the alteration was not validly witnessed for any reason specified in paragraphs (a) to (e) of sub-paragraph (4) below,

the alteration shall be presumed to have been signed by the officer, other Minister or authorised person and by the Minister or office-holder, as the case may be.

(1A) For the purposes of sub-paragraph (1)(b) above, the name and address of the witness may bear to be stated in the alteration itself or in the testing clause or its equivalent.'.

SCHEDULE 3

MODIFICATIONS OF THIS ACT IN RELATION TO SUBSCRIPTION OR SIGNING BY RELEVANT PERSON UNDER SECTION 9

1. For any reference to the subscription or signing of a document by a granter there shall be substituted a reference to such subscription or signing by a relevant person under section 9(1).

2. For section 3(1) there shall be substituted the following subsection—

'(1) Subject to subsections (2) to (6) below, where—

    (a) a document bears to have been subscribed by a relevant person with the authority of a granter of it;

    (b) the document, or the testing clause or its equivalent, states that the document was read to that granter by the relevant person before such subscription or states that it was not so read because the granter made a declaration that he did not wish him to do so;

   (c) the document bears to have been signed by a person as a witness of the relevant person's subscription and the document, or the testing clause or its equivalent, bears to state the name and address of the witness; and

   (d) nothing in the document, or in the testing clause or its equivalent, indicates—

      (i) that it was not subscribed by the relevant person as it bears to have been so subscribed;

      (ii) that the statement mentioned in paragraph (b) above is incorrect; or

      (iii) that it was not validly witnessed for any reason specified in paragraphs (a) to (e) of subsection (4) below (as modified by paragraph 4 of Schedule 3 to this Act),

the document shall be presumed to have been subscribed by the relevant person and the statement so mentioned shall be presumed to be correct.'.

3. In section 3(3) for the words 'subsection (1)(b)' there shall be substituted the words 'subsection (1)(c)'.

4. For section 3(4) therre shall be substituted the following subsection—

'(4) Where, in any proceedings relating to a document in which a question arises as to a relevant person's subscription on behalf of a granter under section 9(1) of this Act, it is established—

   (a) that a signature bearing to be the signature of the witness of the relevant person's subscription is not such a signature, whether by reason of forgery or otherwise;

   (b) that the person who signed the document as the witness of the relevant person's subscription is a person who is named in the document as a granter of it;

   (c) that the person who signed the document as the witness of the relevant person's subscription, at the time of signing—

      (i) did not know the granter on whose behalf the relevant person had so subscribed;

      (ii) was under the age of 16 years; or

      (iii) was mentally incapable of acting as a witness;

   (d) that the person who signed the document, purporting to be the witness of the relevant person's subscription, did not see him subscribe it;

   (dd) that the person who signed the document as the witness of the relevant person's subscription did not witness the granting of authority by the granter concerned to the relevant person to subscribe the document on his behalf or did not witness the reading of the document to the granter by the relevant person or the declaration that the granter did not wish him to do so;

   (e) that the person who signed the document as the witness of the relevant person's subscription did not sign the document after him or that such subscription and signature were not one continuous process;

(f) that the name or address of such a witness was added after the document was founded on or registered as mentioned in subsection (3)(a) above or is erroneous in any material respect; or

(g) in the case of a testamentary document consisting of more than one sheet, that a signature on any sheet bearing to be the signature of the relevant person is not such a signature, whether by reason of forgery or otherwise,

then, for the purposes of those proceedings, there shall be no presumption that the document has been subscribed by the relevant person on behalf of the granter concerned.'.

5. In section 3(6) the words 'or acknowledgement' in both places where they occur shall be omitted.

6. Section 3(7) shall be omitted.

7. For section 4(1) there shall be substituted the following subsection—

   '(1) Where—

   (a) a document bears to have been subscribed by a relevant person under section 9(1) of this Act on behalf of a granter of it; but

   (b) there is no presumption under section 3 of this Act (as modified by paragraph 2 of Schedule 3 to this Act) that the document has been subscribed by that person or that the procedure referred to section 3(1)(b) of this Act as so modified was followed,

   then, if the court, on an application being made to it by any person who has an interest in the document, is satisfied that the document was so subscribed by the relevant person with the authority of the granter and that the relevant person read the document to the granter before subscription or did not so read it because the granter declared that he did not wish him to do so, it shall—

   (i) cause the document to be endorsed with a certificate to that effect; or

   (ii) where the document has already been registered in the Books of Council and Session or in sheriff court books, grant decree to that effect.'.

8. At the end of section 4(5)(a) there shall be added the following words—

   'and that the procedure referred to in section 3(1)(b) of this Act as modified by paragraph 2 of Schedule 3 to this Act was followed.'.

9. For paragraph 1(1) of Schedule 1 there shall be substituted the following sub-paragraph—

   '(1) Subject to sub-paragraphs (2) to (6) below, where—

   (a) an alteration to a document bears to have been signed by a relevant person with the authority of a granter of the document;

    (b) the document or alteration, or the testing clause or its equivalent, states that the alteration was read to that granter by the relevant person before such signature or states that the alteration was not so read because the granter made a declaration that he did not wish him to do so;

    (c) the alteration bears to have been signed by a person as a witness of the relevant person's signature and the alteration, or the testing clause or its equivalent, bears to state the name and address of the witness; and

    (d) nothing in the document or alteration, or in the testing clause or its equivalent, indicates—

        (i) that the alteration was not signed by the relevant person as it bears to have been so signed;

        (ii) that the statement mentioned in paragraph (b) above is incorrect; or

        (iii) that the alteration was not validly witnessed for any reason specified in paragraphs (a) to (e) of sub-paragraph (4) below (as modified by paragraph 11 of Schedule 3 to this Act),

the alteration shall be presumed to have been signed by the relevant person and the statement so mentioned shall be presumed to be correct.'.

10. In paragraph 1(3) of Schedule 1 for the words 'sub-paragraph (1)(b)' there shall be substituted the words 'sub-paragraph (1)(c)'.

11. For paragraph 1(4) of Schedule 1 there shall be substituted the following sub-paragraph—

'(4) Where, in any proceedings relating to an alteration to a document in which a question arises as to a relevant person's signature on behalf of a granter under section 9(1) of this Act, it is established—

    (a) that a signature bearing to be the signature of the witness of the relevant person's signature is not such a signature, whether by reason of forgery or otherwise;

    (b) that the person who signed the alteration as the witness of the relevant person's signature is a person who is named in the document as a granter of it;

    (c) that the person who signed the alteration as the witness of the relevant person's signature, at the time of signing—

        (i) did not know the granter on whose behalf the relevant person had so signed;

        (ii) was under the age of 16 years; or

        (iii) was mentally incapable of acting as a witness;

    (d) that the person who signed the alteration, purporting to be the witness of the relevant person's signature, did not see him sign it;

    (dd) that the person who signed the alteration as the witness of the relevant person's signature did not witness the granting of authority by the granter concerned to the relevant person to sign the alteration on his behalf or did not witness the reading of the alteration to the granter by the relevant person or the declaration that the granter did not wish him to do so;

(e) that the person who signed the alteration as the witness of the relevant person's signature did not sign the alteration after him or that the signing of the alteration by the granter and the witness was not one continuous process;

(f) that the name or address of such a witness was added after the alteration was founded on or registered as mentioned in sub-paragraph (3)(a) above or is erroneous in any material respect; or

(g) in the case of an alteration to a testamentary document consisting of more than one sheet, that a signature on any sheet of the alteration bearing to be the signature of the relevant person is not such a signature, whether by reason of forgery or otherwise,

then, for the purposes of those proceedings, there shall be no presumption that the alteration has been signed by the relevant person on behalf of the granter concerned.'.

12. In paragraph 1(6) of Schedule 1 the words 'or the acknowledgement of his signature' and the words 'or acknowledgement' shall be omitted.

13. Paragraph 1(7) of Schedule 1 shall be omitted.

14. For paragraph 2(1) of Schedule 1 there shall be substituted the following sub-paragraph—

'(1) Where—

(a) an alteration to a document bears to have been signed by a relevant person under section 9(1) of this Act on behalf of a granter of the document; but

(b) there is no presumption under paragraph 1 of Schedule 1 to this Act (as modified by paragraph 9 of Schedule 3 to this Act) that the alteration has been signed by that person or that the procedure referred to in paragraph 1(1)(b) of Schedule 1 to this Act as so modified was followed,

then, if the court, on an application being made to it by any person who has an interest in the document, is satisfied that the alteration was so signed by the relevant person with the authority of the granter and that the relevant person read the alteration to the granter before signing or did not so read it because the granter declared that he did not wish him to do so, it shall—

(i) cause the document to be endorsed with a certificate to that effect; or

(ii) where the document has already been registered in the Books of Council and Session or in sheriff court books, grant decree to that effect.'.

15. At the end of paragraph 2(5)(a) of Schedule 1 there shall be added the following words—

'and that the procedure referred to in paragraph 1(1)(b) of Schedule 1 to this Act as modified by paragraph 9 of Schedule 3 to this Act was followed.'.

SCHEDULE 4

MINOR AND CONSEQUENTIAL AMENDMENTS

General adaptation

1.—(1) Any reference in any other enactment to a probative document shall, in relation to a document executed after the commencement of this Act, be construed as a reference to a document in relation to which section 6(2) of this Act applies.

(2) For the purposes of any enactment—

    (a) providing for a document to be executed by a body corporate by affixing its common seal; or

    (b) referring (in whatever terms) to a document so executed,

a document signed or subscribed by or on behalf of the body corporate in accordance with the provisions of the Requirements of Writing (Scotland) Act 1995 shall have effect as if so executed.

Specific enactments

Lands Clauses Consolidation (Scotland) Act 1845

2. In Schedules (A) and (B) to the Lands Clauses Consolidation (Scotland) Act 1845 at the end of each of the forms there shall be added—

'Note – Subscription of the document by the granter of it will be sufficient for the document to be formally valid, but witnessing of it may be necessary or desirable for other purposes (see the Requirements of Writing (Scotland) Act 1995).'.

Infeftment Act 1845

3. In Schedules (A) and (B) to the Infeftment Act 1845 for the words from 'In witness' to the end there shall be substituted the words 'Testing clause+

+Note – Subscription of the document by the granter of it will be sufficient for the document to be formally valid, but witnessing of it may be necessary or desirable for other purposes (see the Requirements of Writing (Scotland) Act 1995).'.

Commissioners Clauses Act 1847

4. At the end of section 59 of the Commissioners Clauses Act 1847 there shall be added the following subsection—

'(2) This section shall apply to Scotland as if—

    (a) for the words from "by deed under" to "recorded" there were substituted the words—

        "by a document—

        (a) if they are a corporation, subscribed in accordance with section 7 of, and paragraph 5 of Schedule 2 to, the Requirements of Writing (Scotland) Act 1995;

    (b) if they are not a corporation, subscribed in accordance with the said section 7 by the commissioners or any two of them acting by the authority of and on behalf of the commissioners;

and a document so subscribed, followed by infeftment duly recorded,";

    (b) for the words from "under such" to "acting" there were substituted the word "subscribed".'.

5. At the end of section 75 of that Act there shall be added the following subsection—

'(2) This section shall apply to Scotland as if for the words "by deed" to "five of them" there were substituted the words—
"in a document—

    (a) which is duly stamped;

    (b) in which the consideration is truly stated; and

    (c) which is subscribed, if the commissioners—

        (i) are a corporation, in accordance with section 7 of, and paragraph 5 of Schedule 2 to, the Requirements of Writing (Scotland) Act 1995;

        (ii) are not a corporation, in accordance with the said section 7 by the commissioners or any five of them,".'.

6. At the end of section 77 of that Act there shall be added the following subsection—

'(2) This section shall apply to Scotland as if for the words "by deed duly stamped" there were substituted the words "in a document which is duly stamped and which is subscribed in accordance with the Requirements of Writing (Scotland) Act 1995.".'.

7. In Schedule (B) to that Act—

    (a) the words from 'or, if the deed' to 'case may be,' are hereby repealed;

    (b) at the end there shall be added the words '[or, if the document is granted under Scots law, insert testing clause+]

    +Note – As regards a document granted under Scots law, subscription of it by the granter will be sufficient for the document to be formally valid, but witnessing of it may be necessary or desirable for other purposes (see the Requirements of Writing (Scotland) Act 1995).'.

8. In Schedule (C) to that Act—

    (a) the words from '[or, if the deed' to 'Scotland,]' are hereby repealed;

    (b) at the end there shall be added the words '[or, if the document is granted under Scots law, insert testing clause+]

    +Note – As regards a document granted under Scots law, subscription of it by the granter will be sufficient for the document to be formally valid, but witnessing of it may be necessary or desirable for other purposes (see the Requirements of Writing (Scotland) Act 1995).'.

Entail Amendment Act 1848

9. In section 50 of the Entail Amendment Act 1848 for the word 'tested' there shall be substituted the word 'subscribed'.
10. In the Schedule to that Act—
    (a) the words 'and of the witnesses subscribing,' are hereby repealed;
    (b) for the words from 'In witness whereof' to the end there shall be substituted the words 'Testing clause+
       +Note – Subscription of the document by the heir of entail in possession and the notary public will be sufficient for the document to be formally valid, but witnessing of it may be necessary or desirable for other purposes (see the Requirements of Writing (Scotland) Act 1995).'.

Ordnance Board Transfer Act 1855

11. At the end of section 5 of the Ordnance Board Transfer Act 1855 there shall be added the following subsection—
    '(2) This section shall apply to Scotland as if for the words from "signing" to "his deed" there were substituted the words "subscribing it in accordance with the Requirements of Writing (Scotland) Act 1995".'

Registration of Leases (Scotland) Act 1857

12. In Schedule (A) to the Registration of Leases (Scotland) Act 1857 for the words 'in common form' there shall be substituted—
    '+
       +Note – Subscription of the document by the granter of it will be sufficient for the document to be formally valid, but witnessing of it may be necessary or desirable for other purposes (see the Requirements of Writing (Scotland) Act 1995).'.
13. In each of Schedules (B), (C), (D), (F), (G) and (H) to that Act after the words 'Testing clause' there shall be inserted '+
       +Note – Subscription of the document by the granter of it will be sufficient for the document to be formally valid, but witnessing of it may be necessary or desirable for other purposes (see the Requirements of Writing (Scotland) Act 1995).'.

Transmission of Moveable Property (Scotland) Act 1862

14. In each of Schedules A and B to the Transmission of Moveable Property (Scotland) Act 1862 for the words from 'In witness whereof' to the end there shall be substituted the words 'Testing clause+
       +Note – Subscription of the document by the granter of it will be sufficient for the document to be formally valid, but witnessing of it may be necessary or desirable for other purposes (see the Requirements of Writing (Scotland) Act 1995).'.
15. In Schedule C to that Act for the words from 'and D' to the end there shall be substituted the words 'Testing clause'.

Titles to Land Consolidation (Scotland) Act 1868

16. In Schedule (B) nos. 1 and 2 and (AA) no. 3 to the Titles to Land Consolidation (Scotland) Act 1868 for the words from 'In witness whereof' to 'usual form]' there shall be substituted the words 'Testing clause+

   +Note – Subscription of the document by the granter of it will be sufficient for the document to be formally valid, but witnessing of it may be necessary or desirable for other purposes (see the Requirements of Writing (Scotland) Act 1995).'.

17. In Schedules (J), (BB) no.1, (CC) nos. 1 and 2 and (OO) to that Act for the words from 'In witness whereof' to the end there shall be substituted the words 'Testing clause+

   +Note – Subscription of the document by the granter of it will be sufficient for the document to be formally valid, but witnessing of it may be necessary or desirable for other purposes (see the Requirements of Writing (Scotland) Act 1995).'.

18. In Schedule (FF) no. 1 to that Act—
   (a) for the words from 'In witness whereof' to 'usual form]' there shall be substituted the words 'Testing clause+';
   (b) at the end there shall be added '+Subscription of the document by the granter of it will be sufficient for the document to be formally valid, but witnessing of it may be necessary or desirable for other purposes (see the Requirements of Writing (Scotland) Act 1995).'.

19. In Schedule (GG) to that Act—
   (a) for the words from 'In witness whereof' to 'I K Witness' there shall be substituted the words 'Testing clause+';
   (b) after Note (b) there shall be inserted—
      '+(c) Subscription of the document by the granter of it will be sufficient for the document to be formally valid, but witnessing of it may be necessary or desirable for other purposes (see the Requirements of Writing (Scotland) Act 1995).'.

20. In Schedule (NN) to that Act—
   (a) for the words from 'In witness whereof' to 'G H Witness' there shall be substituted the words 'Testing clause+';
   (b) at the end there shall be added—
      '+Subscription of the document by the granter if it will be sufficient for the document to be formally valid, but witnessing of it may be necessary or desirable for other purposes (see the Requirements of Writing (Scotland) Act 1995).'.

Conveyancing (Scotland) Act 1874

21. In Schedules C, F, L nos. 1 and 2 and N to the Conveyancing (Scotland) Act 1874 for the words 'In witness whereof [testing clause]' there shall be substituted the words 'Testing clause+

+Note – Subscription of the document by the granter of it will be sufficient for the document to be formally valid, but witnessing of it may be necessary or desirable for other purposes (see the Requirements of Writing (Scotland) Act 1995).'.

22. In Schedule G to that Act—
    (a) for the words 'In witness whereof [testing clause]' there shall be substituted the words 'Testing clause+';
    (b) at the end of the Note there shall be added—
        '+Subscription of the document by the granter of it will be sufficient for the document to be formally valid, but witnessing of it may be necessary or desirable for other purposes (see the Requirements of Writing (Scotland) Act 1995).'.

23. In Schedule M to that Act for the words 'and add testing clause]' there shall be substituted the words 'Testing clause+]
    +Note – Subscription of the document by the granter of it will be sufficient for the document to be formally valid, but witnessing of it may be necessary or desirable for other purposes (see the Requirements of Writing (Scotland) Act 1995).'.

Colonial Stock Act 1877

24. At the end of subsection (1) of section 4 of the Colonial Stock Act 1877 there shall be added the words 'or, in relation to Scotland, subscribed in accordance with section 7 of the Requirements of Writing (Scotland) Act 1995.'.

25. At the end of section 6 of that Act there shall be added the following subsection—
    '(2) This section shall have effect in relation to Scotland as if for the words from "given" to "attested" there were substituted the words "subscribed by the person not under disability in accordance with section 7 of the Requirements of Writing (Scotland) Act 1995.".'.

Colonial Stock Act 1892

26. After subsection (2) of section 2 of the Colonial Stock Act 1892 there shall be added the following subsection—
    '(2A) This section shall have effect in relation to Scotland as if—
        (a) in subsection (1) for the words from "deed according" to "parties" there were substituted the words "a document in the form set out in the Schedule to this Act or to the like effect and the document as executed";
        (b) in subsection (2) for the words "by deed" there were substituted the words "under this section".'

27. At the end of the Schedule to that Act there shall be added the words '[If the document is granted under the law of Scotland, for the words from "Witness our hands" to the end substitute "[Testing clause+

+Note – Subscription of the document by the granter of it will be sufficient for the document to be formally valid, but witnessing of it may be necessary or desirable for other purposes (see the Requirements of Writing (Scotland) Act 1995).]"]'.

Feudal Casualties (Scotland) Act 1914

28. In each of Schedules B and C to the Feudal Casualties (Scotland) Act 1914—
    (a) for the words 'In witness whereof' there shall be substituted the words 'Testing clause'; and
    (b) at the end of the Note there shall be added the words 'Subscription of the document by the granter of it will be sufficient for the document to be formally valid, but witnessing of it may be necessary or desirable for other purposes (see the Requirements of Writing (Scotland) Act 1995).'.

Trusts (Scotland) Act 1921

29. In Schedule A to the Trusts (Scotland) Act 1921—
    (a) for the words '(To be attested)' there shall be substituted the words 'Testing clause+';
    (b) at the end there shall be added—
        +Note – Subscription of the document by the granter of it will be sufficient for the document to be formally valid, but witnessing of it may be necessary or desirable for other purposes (see the Requirements of Writing (Scotland) Act 1995).'.
30. In Schedule B to that Act for the words '(To be attested)' there shall be substituted the words 'Testing clause+
    +Note – Subscription of the document by the granter or granters of it will be sufficient for the document to be formally valid, but witnessing of it may be necessary or desirable for other purposes (see the Requirements of Writing (Scotland) Act 1995).'.

Conveyancing (Scotland) Act 1924

31. In Schedule B to the Conveyancing (Scotland) Act 1924—
    (a) in forms nos. 1 to 6 for the words '[To be attested]' there shall be substituted the words 'Testing clause+';
    (b) at the end of the Notes there shall be added—
        '+Note 8 – Subscription of the document by the notary public (or law agent) on behalf of the granter of it will be sufficient for the document to be formally valid, but witnessing of

it may be necessary or desirable for other purposes (see the Requirements of Writing (Scotland) Act 1995).'.

32. In Schedule E to that Act for the words '[To be attested]' there shall be substituted the words 'Testing clause+
    +Note – Subscription of the document by the granter of it will be sufficient for the document to be formally valid, but witnessing of it may be necessary or desirable for other purposes (see the Requirements of Writing (Scotland) Act 1995).'.

33. In Schedules G and H to that Act for the words '[To be attested]' there shall be substituted the words 'Testing clause+
    +Note – Subscription of the document by the granter of it will be sufficient for the document to be formally valid, but witnessing of it may be necessary or desirable for other purposes (see the Requirements of Writing (Scotland) Act 1995)'.

34. In Schedule K to that Act—
    (a) in forms nos 1 to 7 for the words '[To be attested]' there shall be substituted the words 'Testing clause+';
    (b) at the end of the notes there shall be added—
        '+Note 5 – Subscription of the document by the granter of it will be sufficient for the document to be formally valid, but witnessing of it may be necessary or desirable for other purposes (see the Requirements of Writing (Scotland) Act 1995).'.

35. In Schedule L to that Act, in form 4, for the words '[To be attested]' there shall be substituted the words 'Testing clause+
    +Note – Subscription of the document by the notary public or law agent on behalf of the granter of it will be sufficient for the document to be formally valid, but witnessing of it may be necessary or desirable for other purposes (see the Requirements of Writing (Scotland) Act 1995).'.

36. In Schedule N to that Act for the words '[To be attested]' there shall be substituted the words 'Testing clause+
    +Note – Subscription of the document by the granter of it will be sufficient for the document to be formally valid, but witnessing of it may be necessary or desirable for other purposes (see the Requirements of Writing (Scotland) Act 1995).'.

Long Leases (Scotland) Act 1954

37. In the Fourth Schedule to the Long Leases (Scotland) Act 1954—
    (a) for the words '[To be attested]' there shall be substituted the words – 'Testing clause+;'
    (b) at the end of the Notes there shall be added—
        '+4 Subscription of the feu contract by the parties to it will be sufficient for the contract to be formally valid, but witnessing of it may be necessary or desirable for other purposes (see the Requirements of Writing (Scotland) Act 1995).'.

Succession (Scotland) Act 1964

38. At the end of section 21 of the Succession (Scotland) Act 1964 there shall be added the following subsection—

'(2) This section shall not apply to a testamentary document executed after the commencement of the Requirements of Writing (Scotland) Act 1995.'.

39. After section 21 of that Act there shall be inserted the following section—

'Evidence as to testamentary documents in commissary proceedings

21A. Confirmation of an executor to property disposed of in a testamentary document executed after the commencement of the Requirements of Writing (Scotland) Act 1995 shall not be granted unless the formal validity of the document is governed—

(a) by Scots law and the document is presumed under section 3 or 4 of that Act to have been subscribed by the granter so disposing of that property; or

(b) by a law other than Scots law and the court is satisfied that the document is formally valid according to the law governing such validity.'.

40. For section 32 of that Act there shall be substituted the following section—

'Certain testamentary dispositions to be formally valid.

32.—(1) For the purpose of any question arising as to entitlement, by virtue of a testamentary disposition, to any relevant property or to any interest therein, the disposition shall be treated as valid in respect of the formalities of execution.

(2) Subsection (1) above is without prejudice to any right to challenge the validity of the testamentary disposition on the ground of forgery or on any other ground of essential invalidity.

(3) In this section "relevant property" means property disposed of in the testamentary disposition in respect of which—

(a) confirmation has been granted; or

(b) probate, letters of administration or other grant of representation—

(i) has been issued, and has noted the domicile of the deceased to be, in England and Wales or Northern Ireland; or

(ii) has been issued outwith the United Kingdom and had been sealed in Scotland under section 2 of the Colonial Probates Act 1892.'.

41. In Schedule 1 to that Act for the words '[To be attested by two witnesses] [Signature of A B]' there shall be substituted the words 'Testing clause+
     +Note – Subscription of the document by the granter of it will be sufficient for the document to be formally valid, but witnessing of it may be necessary or desirable for other purposes (see the Requirements of Writing (Scotland) Act 1995).'.

Industrial and Provident Societies Act 1965

42. In Schedule 3 to the Industrial and Provident Societies Act 1965 in each of Forms C, D and E for the words from 'Signed' to the end there shall be substituted the words 'Testing clause+
     +Note – Subscription of the document by the granter of it will be sufficient for the document to be formally valid, but witnessing of it may be necessary or desirable for other purposes (see the Requirements of Writing (Scotland) Act 1995).'.

43. In Schedule 4 to that Act, in Form C for the words from 'Signed' to the end there shall be substituted the words 'Testing clause+
     +Note – Subscription of the document by the cautioner will be sufficient for the document to be formally valid, but witnessing of it may be necessary or desirable for other purposes (see the Requirements of Writing (Scotland) Act 1995).'.

Conveyancing and Feudal Reform (Scotland) Act 1970

44. In Schedule 2 to the Conveyancing and Feudal Reform (Scotland) Act 1970—
     (a) in Forms A and B for the words '[To be attested]' there shall be substituted the words 'Testing clause+';
     (b) at the end of the Notes there shall be added—
          '+Note 8 – Subscription of the document by the granter of it will be sufficient for the document to be formally valid, but witnessing of it may be necessary or desirable for other purposes (see the Requirements of Writing (Scotland) Act 1995).'.

45. In Schedule 4 to that Act—
     (a) in form A and forms C to F for the words '[To be attested]' there shall be substituted the words 'Testing clause+';
     (b) at the end of the Notes there shall be added—
          '+Note 7 – Subscription of the document by the granter of it, or in the case of form E the granter and the consenter to the variation, will be sufficient for the document to be formally valid, but witnessing of it may be necessary or desirable for other purposes (see the Requirements of Writing (Scotland) Act 1995).'.

46. In Schedule 5 to that Act, in form D—
     (a) in nos 1 and 2 for the words '[To be attested]' there shall be substituted the words 'Testing clause+';
     (b) at the end there shall be added—

'+Note – Subscription of the document by the granter of it will be sufficient for the document to be formally valid, but witnessing of it may be necessary or desirable for other purposes (see the Requirements of Writing (Scotland) Act 1995).'.

47. In Schedule 9 to that Act—

   (a) for the words '[To be attested]' there shall be substituted the words 'Testing clause+';

   (b) at the end of the Notes there shall be added—

   '+Note 4 – Subscription of the document by the granter of it will be sufficient for the document to be formally valid, but witnessing of it may be necessary or desirable for other purposes (see the Requirements of Writing (Scotland) Act 1995).'.

Petroleum and Submarine Pipe-lines Act 1975

48. At the end of section 18(5)(b) of the Petroleum and Submarine Pipelines Act 1975 there shall be added the words 'or, as respects Scotland, by an instrument subscribed by the Secretary of State and the licensee in accordance with the Requirements of Writing (Scotland) Act 1995.'.

Patents Act 1977

49. In section 31(6) of the Patents Act 1977 for the words from 'probative' to the end there shall be substituted the words 'subscribed in accordance with the Requirements of Writing (Scotland) Act 1995.'.

Oil and Gas (Enterprise) Act 1982

50. At the end of section 19(2) of the Oil and Gas (Enterprise) Act 1982 there shall be added the words 'or, as respects Scotland, by an instrument subscribed by the Secretary of State and the licensee in accordance with the Requirements of Writing (Scotland) Act 1995.'.

Companies Act 1985

51. For section 36B of the Companies Act 1985 there shall be substituted the following section—

'Execution of documents by companies.   36B.—(1) Notwithstanding the provisions of any enactment, a company need not have a company seal.

(2) For the purposes of any enactment—

   (a) providing for a document to be executed by a company by affixing its common seal; or

   (b) referring (in whatever terms) to a document so executed,

   a document signed or subscribed by or on behalf of the company in accordance with the provisions of the Requirements of Writing (Scotland) Act 1995 shall have effect as if so executed.

(3) In this section "enactment" includes an enactment contained in a statutory instrument.'.

52. At the end of section 38 of that Act there shall be added the following subsection—
    '(3) This section does not extend to Scotland.'.
53. In section 39 of that Act—
    (a) after subsection (2) there shall be inserted the following subsection—
       '(2A) Subsection (2) does not extend to Scotland.';
    (b) in subsection (3) after the words 'common seal' there shall be inserted the words 'or as respects Scotland by writing subscribed in accordance with the Requirements of Writing (Scotland) Act 1995'.
54. Section 40 of that Act shall become subsection (1) of that section and at the end there shall be added the following subsection—
    '(2) Nothing in this section shall affect the right of a company registered in Scotland to subscribe such securities and documents in accordance with the Requirements of Writing (Scotland) Act 1995.'.
55. Section 186 of that Act shall become subsection (1) of that section and at the end there shall be added the following subsection—
    '(2) Without prejudice to subsection (1), as respects Scotland a certificate specifying any shares held by a member and subscribed by the company in accordance with the Requirements of Writing (Scotland) Act 1995 is, unless the contrary is shown, sufficient evidence of his title to the shares.'.
56. In section 188 of that Act in subsection (2) after the words 'common seal' there shall be inserted the words '(or, in the case of a company registered in Scotland, subscribed in accordance with the Requirements of Writing (Scotland) Act 1955)'.

Companies Consolidation (Consequential Provisions) Act 1985

57. At the end of section 11 of the Companies Consolidation (Consequential Provisions) Act 1985 there shall be added the following subsection—
    '(3) The foregoing provisions of this section are without prejudice to the right of a company to subscribe such securities and documents in accordance with the Requirements of Writing (Scotland) Act 1995.'.

Insolvency Act 1986

58. In section 53 of the Insolvency Act 1986—
    (a) in subsection (1) for the words 'a validly executed instrument in writing' there shall be substituted the words 'an instrument subscribed in accordance with the Requirements of Writing (Scotland) Act 1995';
    (b) for subsection (4) there shall be substituted the following subsection—

'(4) If the receiver is to be appointed by the holders of a series of secured debentures, the instrument of appointment may be executed on behalf of the holders of the floating charge by any person authorised by resolution of the debenture-holders to execute the instrument.'.

Housing (Scotland) Act 1987

59. In section 53(1) of the Housing (Scotland) Act 1987 for the words from 'probative' to the end there shall be substituted the words 'subscribed by the parties in accordance with the Requirements of Writing (Scotland) Act 1995.'.
60. In section 54(6) of that Act for the words 'probative or holograph of the parties' there shall be substituted the words 'subscribed by the parties in accordance with the Requirements of Writing (Scotland) Act 1995,'.

SCHEDULE 5

REPEALS

Chapter	Short title	Extent of repeal
1540 c 37 (S).	The Subscription of Deeds Act 1540.	The whole Act.
1579 c 18 (S).	The Subscription of Deeds Act 1579.	The whole Act.
1672 c 47 (S).	The Lyon King of Arms Act 1672.	The words from 'And his Maiestie with consent' to 'contraveiners heirof'.
1681 c 5 (S).	The Subscription of Deeds Act 1681.	The whole Act.
1696 c 15 (S).	The Deeds Act 1696.	The whole Act.
1696 c 25 (S).	The Blank Bonds and Trusts Act 1696.	The whole Act.
1698 c 4 (S).	The Registration Act 1698.	The whole Act.
10 & 11 Vict c 16.	The Commissioners Clauses Act 1847.	In Section 56, the words from '(that is to say,)' to 'discharge the same' where they first occur. In Schedule (B), the words from 'or, if the deed' to 'case may be,'. In Schedule (C), the words from '[or, if the deed' to 'Scotland,]'.
11 & 12 Vict c 36.	The Entail Amendment Act 1848.	In the Schedule the words 'and of the witnesses subscribing,'.

Chapter	Short title	Extent of repeal
19 & 20 Vict c 60.	The Mercantile Law Amendment Act, Scotland 1856.	Section 6.
31 & 32 Vict c 101.	The Titles to Land Consolidation (Scotland) Act 1868.	Sections 139 and 149.
37 & 38 Vict c 94.	The Conveyancing (Scotland) Act 1874.	Sections 38 to 41. Schedule I.
7 Edw 7 c 51.	The Sheriff Courts (Scotland) Act 1907.	In section 35 the words 'either holograph or attested by one witness'. In Schedule 1, paragraph 67 and in the Appendix in Form M the words from 'If not holograph' to the end of the form.
4 & 5 Geo 5 c 48.	The Feudal Casualties (Scotland) Act 1914.	In section 8 the words 'which need not be tested or holograph'.
14 & 15 Geo 5 c 27.	The Conveyancing (Scotland) Act 1924.	Section 18. Section I.
23 & 24 Geo 5 c 44.	The Church of Scotland (Property and Endowments) (Amendment) Act 1933.	Section 13.
2 & 3 Geo 6 c 20.	The Reorganisation of Offices (Scotland) Act 1939.	In section 1(8) the words from 'and any such' to the end.
1959 c 40.	The Deer (Scotland) Act 1959.	In Schedule 1, paragraphs 12 and 13.
1963 c 18.	The Stock Transfer Act 1963.	Section 2(4).
1965 c 12.	The Industrial and Provident Societies Act 1965.	In section 34(5)(a), in the definition of 'receipt' the words from 'signed by two members' to 'as such'. Section 36.
1967 c 10.	The Forestry Act 1967.	Section 39(5).
1968 c 16.	The New Towns (Scotland) Act 1968.	In Schedule 2, paragraphs 10 and 11.
1970 c 35.	The Conveyancing and Feudal Reform (Scotland) Act 1970.	Section 44.
1973 c 52.	The Prescription and Limitation (Scotland) Act 1973.	Section 5(2). In Schedule 1, paragraphs 2(c), 3 and 4(b).

Chapter	Short title	Extent of repeal
1973 c 65.	The Local Government (Scotland) Act 1973.	Section 194, other than subsection (2). In Schedule 8, paragraph 5.
1978 c 29.	The National Health Service (Scotland) Act 1978.	In section 79(1A) the words from 'and where' to the end of the subsection. In Schedule 1, paragraphs 9 and 10. In Schedule 5, paragraphs 10 and 11.
1980 c 46.	The Solicitors (Scotland) Act 1980.	In Schedule 1, paragraph 12.
1985 c 6.	The Companies Act 1985.	In section 2(6) the words from 'and that' to the end. In section 7(3)(c) the words from '(which attestation' to the end. Section 426(3).
1985 c 16.	The National Heritage (Scotland) Act 1985.	In Schedule 1, paragraphs 8 and 19.
1986 c 47.	The Legal Aid (Scotland) Act 1986.	In Schedule 1, paragraph 14.
1988 c 43.	The Housing (Scotland) Act 1988.	In Schedule 1, paragraphs 18 and 19.
1990 c 40.	The Law Reform (Miscellaneous Provisions) (Scotland) Act 1990.	Section 72. Section 75(6). In Schedule 8, paragraph 33.
1990 c 35.	The Enterprise and New Towns (Scotland) Act 1990.	In Schedule 1, paragraph 23.
1991 c 28.	The Natural Heritage (Scotland) Act 1991.	In Schedule 1, paragraph 18.
1993 c 44.	The Crofters (Scotland) Act 1993.	In Schedule 1, paragraphs 14 and 15.
1994 c 39.	The Local Government etc. (Scotland) Act 1994.	In section 172(4), paragraph (h). In Schedule 3, paragraph 11. In Schedule 5, in Part II, paragraph 8. In Schedule 7, paragraph 17. In Schedule 12, paragraph 13. In Schedule 13, paragraph 92(60).

Index

Act of 1540 . . . 1.08
Act of 1555 . . . 1.08
Act of 1579 . . . 1.08
Act of 1584 . . . 1.08
Act of 1593 . . . 1.08
Administrator
execution of deeds by, 2.10, 4.04
Alterations
authentication, practical
considerations, 3.42
generally, 1.14, 2.18–2.21, 3.39
holograph writings, to, 2.36
self-proving status of, 3.40
testamentary writings, in, 2.25,
3.41
testing clause, 3.42
Annexations
notarial execution, in, 3.35
self-proving status and, 3.31
subscription of, 2.03, 3.27
Attestation
alternative to, 1.14, 3.31
defective, 2.14, 3.25
exemptions from requirement for,
3.29
meaning, 1.07
probativity and, 1.06, 1.14
self-proving status and, 3.31
when required, 3.29
Attorney
execution of deed by, 3.17
Authentication statutes
criticisms of, 1.13
generally, 1.06–1.11, 2.02
probativity and, 1.06
rationale of, 1.07, 1.12
repeal of, 1.07, 1.15

Bank of Scotland
execution of deeds by, 4.07
Blind person
execution of deed by, 2.31
subscription by, 3.32
witness, as, 3.21
Body corporate
execution of deed by, 4.07

Books of Council and Session
documents registered in, 3.29
Building society
execution of deeds, by, 2.09

Company
common seal of, 2.10, 5.06
described incorrectly, 2.11
execution of deeds by—
authorised person, 4.04
generally, 2.10, 4.03
judicial factor, and, 4.05
self-proving status, 4.04
Confirmation
grant of, 5.05
Contract, obligation or trust
improperly constituted, 3.03
rei interventus, conclusion by, 3.09
Conveyancing
meaning, 1.01
Corporate body
execution of deeds by, 2.11

Deed
adopted in separate deed, 2.39
alterations to, 1.14, 2.18, 2.20, 2.21,
3.39
blanks in, 2.22, 2.23
erasures in, 2.19, 3.41
execution of, *see* EXECUTION OF DEEDS
material alteration, 2.20
minor alteration, 2.21
pagination, 1.10, 2.02
partly printed, 2.24
reduction of, 2.14
registration required, 3.29
Deeds Act 1696 . . . 1.09
Designation
witness, of, 1.09, 3.19
writer, of, 1.08, 1.09
Document
See DEED

Erasure, 2.19, 3.41
Error
testing clause, in, 2.17

Essential validity
formal validity distinguished, 1.02
Execution of deeds
administrator, by, 2.10, 4.04
Bank of Scotland, by, 4.07
building society, by, 2.09
company, by, 2.10, 2.11, 4.03–4.05
corporate body, by, 2.11, 4.07
date and place of, 3.24
defect in—
  curable defect, 2.30
  informality, 2.27
  major defect, 2.29
  minor defect, 2.28
  onus of proof, 2.14, 2.27
  trivial defect, 2.26, 2.28
early examples, 1.07
foundation of modern practice, 1.08
forgery and fraud, 1.07, 1.12,
  1.13
friendly society, by, 4.07
inessentials, 2.04
informality in, 2.27
judicial factor, by, 4.05
limited company, by, 1.07
local authority, by, 2.08, 4.06
mark or cross, by, 1.08
Minister of the Crown, by, 4.08
outwith Scotland, 2.41–2.44
partnership, by, 2.07, 4.02
receiver, by, 2.10, 4.04
requirements pre-1995 Act, *see*
  Chapter 2
requirements post-1995 Act, *see*
  Chapters 3–5
statutory body, by, 2.11
trade union, by, 4.07
university, by, 4.07
Extrinsic evidence
inadmissibility, 1.09

Foreign deed
moveables, relating to, 2.42
privilege of, 2.41–2.44
registration of, 3.29
Scottish heritage, relating to, 2.42
testamentary writing, 2.43, 2.44
Forgery
attempts to prevent, 1.07, 1.11, 1.12
witness's signature, of, 3.20
Formal validity
abolition, 1.13
essential validity distinguished, 1.02
generally, 2.01
governed by foreign law, 3.29

Friendly society
execution of deeds by, 4.07

Granter
acting in different capacities, 3.14
illiterate, 1.08, 3.32
more than one, 3.13, 3.31
subscription of—
  pre-1995 Act, 2.05–2.11
  post-1995 Act, 3.12–3.17, 3.31.
  See also SUBSCRIPTION
Gratuitous unilateral obligation
creation of, 1.14, 3.02

Heritage
contract or obligation in, 3.02
partnership property, as, 4.02
Scottish, *lex loci situs*, 2.42
Holograph writings
abolition, 1.14, 3.38
alteration to, 2.36
generally, 2.35
in part, 2.37
missives and, 1.14, 3.38
privileged status of, 1.03
requirements of, 2.38
Homologation
abolition, 1.14, 3.03
personal bar and, 3.08

Illiterate granter
notarial execution for, 1.08, 3.32
In re mercatoria, **writings in**
abolition, 1.14, 3.38
privileged status of, 1.03
Informal writings
adoption of, 2.39
Interest in land
annexation to deed, 3.27, 3.31
lex loci situs for, 2.42
meaning, 3.10
writing required, 1.14

Judicial factor
execution of deeds by, 4.05

Land Register
deeds registered in, 3.30
Law reform
criticisms of proposals, 1.15
Scottish Law Commission and, 1.14
Limited company
execution of deeds by, 1.07

Local authority
execution of deeds by, 2.08, 4.06
proper officer of, 4.06

Man
mode of signature, 2.06
Married woman
mode of signature, 2.06
Minister of the Crown
execution of deeds by, 4.08
Missives
holograph writing and,1.14, 3.38
requirement of writing, 3.02
Moveables
deed for executed outwith Scotland,
2.42

Natural person
execution of deeds by, 2.01, 3.31
Notarial execution
authentication statutes, under, 1.08,
2.02
benefit to executor from, 2.31, 3.36
blind person, for, 3.32
disqualifying interest, 2.31, 3.36
generally, 2.31, 3.32
illiterate person, for, 1.08, 3.32
informality in, 2.33
post-1995 Act, 3.32–3.36
pre-1995 Act, 1.08, 2.31, 2.32
procedure, 2.32, 3.35
'relevant person' for, 3.32
testamentary writing and, 3.32
to whom available, 1.08, 2.31, 3.34
unico contextu, 2.32
who may execute, 2.31, 3.33
witness to, 3.32
Non-natural persons
execution of deeds by, 4.01

Obligationes literis
abolition, 3.38
categories, 1.05
meaning, 1.04, 1.05
Obligations
categories of, 1.04

Page
numbering of, 1.10, 1.11, 2.02
signature on every, 2.03
Partnership
execution of deed by, 2.07, 4.02
Peer
signature, mode of, 2.06, 3.15

Personal bar
homologation and, 3.08
meaning, 3.08n
requirements for, 3.03–3.07
knowledge and acquiescence, 3.06
material consequences, 3.07
preceding contract, 3.04
reliance on the agreement, 3.05
statutory, introduction of, 1.14, 3.03
Prescription, 5.02
Privileged writings
abolition of special status, 1.14, 3.38
generally, 1.03, 2.34
See also HOLOGRAPH WRITINGS; IN RE
MERCATORIA, WRITINGS IN;
OBLIGATIONES LITERIS
Probativity
1995 Act, under, 3.02, 3.18–3.31. *See*
also SELF-PROVING STATUS;
SUBSCRIPTION; WITNESS
attestation and, 1.06
challenging, 1.02
concept of, 1.06
generally, 1.14
inadmissibility of extrinsic evidence,
1.09
meaning, 1.02, 1.07
missives, of, 1.15, 3.38
requirements of, 1.08
self-proving status, and, 3.08, 5.03
Proof by writ or oath
abolition of, 3.38

Receiver
appointment of, 5.06
execution of deeds by, 2.10, 4.04
Register of Sasines
recording in, 3.29
Registration or recording
documents requiring, 3.29
expressly permitted, 3.29
interest in land, of, 3.27
Land Register, in, 3.30
special register, in, 3.29
testamentary writing, of, 3.29
Rei interventus
abolition, 1.14, 3.03
application of doctrine, 3.09
requirement of writing, and, 3.09
Repealed provisions, 5.02

Sealing, 1.08
Scottish Law Commission
proposals for reform, 1.14

Self-proving status
alteration, of, 3.40
application for, 3.28
certification of, 3.28
deed executed by company, 4.03,
  4.04
deed notarially executed and, 3.32
effect of certificate of, 3.28
evidential requirements, 3.28
loss of, 3.21
non-natural persons and, 4.01
requirements under 1995 Act, 3.18,
  3.30, 3.31
subscription as, 3.18
unico contextu rule and, 3.23
Signature
forged, 3.20
granter, of, 2.05–2.11, 3.12–3.17
initials, by, 2.06, 3.12
man, of, 2.06
mark, by, 2.06, 3.12
married woman, of, 2.06
mechanical means by, 2.06
nickname, by, 3.12
peer, of, 2.06, 3.15
position of granter's, 3.13, 3.14
Sovereign, of, 2.05, 3.15
style of, 2.06–2.11, 3.12, 3.31
voluntary nature of, 2.06, 3.16
witness, of—
  forged, 3.20
  name and designation, 3.19
  style of, 2.12, 3.26
  time of signing, 2.13, 3.23
See also SUBSCRIPTION
Sovereign
signature of, 2.05, 3.15
Stamp duty, 2.04
Statutory body
execution of deeds by, 2.11
Subscription
Act of 1540, and, 1.08
Act of 1555 and, 1.08
annexation, of, 3.27
attestation of, 1.06
attorney, by, 3.17
company, by, 2.10, 4.03, 4.04
date and place of, 2.04, 3.24
every page, on, 2.03
granter, by, 1.08, 2.02, 2.03, 2.05–
  2.11, 3.02, 3.12–3.17, 3.31
natural persons, by, 2.01
presumption of, 3.28
requirement for, 3.11
self-proving status and, 3.18

Subscription—*contd*
wills and testamentary writings, of,
  1.10, 2.03, 3.11
witnesses, of, 1.08, 2.12–2.14, 3.18–3.23
See also SIGNATURE
Subscription of Deeds Act 1681 . . .
  1.08
Superscription
Sovereign, of, 2.05, 3.15

Testamentary writing
additions or interlineations, 2.25
alterations in, 2.25, 3.39, 3.40
creation of, 3.02
erasures, 2.25, 3.41
executed abroad, 2.43, 2.44
executed on board aircraft or ship, 2.44
formal validity, 5.05
holograph, 2.37, 5.05
registration of, 3.29
self-proving status, 3.18
signature cancelled, 2.25
subscription of, 1.11, 2.03, 3.11, 3.31
substituted words, 2.25
Testing clause
alterations noted in, 3.42
amendment of, 5.03
errors in, 2.17
form of, 3.37
generally, 2.15
retention of, 3.37
time of completion, 2.16
witness mentioned in, 3.19
Trade union
execution of deed by, 4.07
Trust
constitution of, 1.14, 3.02

Unico contextu **rule**
notarial execution and, 2.32
subscription by witness and, 3.23
University
execution of deed by, 4.07

Will
See TESTAMENTARY WRITING
Witness
Act of 1540, and, 1.08
act of witnessing, 3.22
blind person as, 3.21
described as, 2.04
mandate of, 2.13, 3.23
name and designation, 1.09, 2.02,
  2.03, 3.19, 3.31
notarial execution, to, 3.32
persons competent as, 2.12, 3.21

Witness—*contd*
persons not competent as, 2.12, 3.21
probativity and, 3.18
requirement for, 1.08, 1.09, 2.02, 2.03,
    3.31
signature of—
    forged, 3.20
    style of, 2.12, 3.26
    time of, 2.13

Witness—*contd*
subscription of, 1.08, 2.03
unico contextu rule, 3.23
Writing
missives and, 3.02
not required, 3.01
requirements of, 1.13, 3.02
Writings *in re mercatoria*, *See* IN RE
    MERCATORIA, WRITINGS IN